Cleaning Out Your Mental Closet

Transforming Negative Emotions

Cleaning Out Your Mental Closet

TRANSFORMING NEGATIVE EMOTIONS

Chuck Cerling

Harold Shaw Publishers
Wheaton, Illinois

All Scripture quotations are taken from *The Living Bible* unless otherwise noted.

Copyright © 1987 by Chuck Cerling

ISBN 0-87788-127-8

Library of Congress Cataloging-in-Publication Data
Cerling, Charles E.
Cleaning out your mental closet
1. Emotions.   2. Imaginary conversations.
3. Christian life—1961-   I. Title.
BF561.C47   1987   152.4   86-31580
ISBN 0-87788-127-8

---

98 97 96 95 94 93 92 91 90 89 88 87

10 9 8 7 6 5 4 3 2 1

To my wife, Geri

CONTENTS

CONTENTS

1

Talk to Myself? Are You Kidding?

AS MY WIFE, GERI, worked around the bedroom, making the bed, picking up T-shirts and scattered shoes, and dusting and vacuuming, she carried on a running conversation with herself. Peter, our youngest son, heard her talking and wandered into the room to see who she was talking with. Seeing no one he turned and asked, "Mommy, who are you talking to?" He was puzzled because she was alone.

Geri's conversation reveals a common human behavior—something I call *Self-Talk*. The only difference is that she talked *out loud* to herself. Whether it's conscious or not, we all carry on a silent running conversation with ourselves about what we see, feel, hear, taste, or do. We talk with ourselves about the present, the past, and the future. We talk about ideas, events, people, and feelings. And the self-talk we carry on with ourselves regarding who we are, what others think of us, the value of our goals and personhood is what shapes our personalities and views. What you say to yourself consciously or subconsciously reinforces what you think and how you feel about yourself—for good and for bad.

This running conversation is always racing around inside our heads. It's both high speed and seemingly beyond our control. Many times unbidden thoughts spring into our minds and harrass us.

Because our thoughts come in both words and pictures, we talk to ourselves at thousands of words per minute. That's amazing—and also frightening. But when we consciously decide to take control of our thoughts, we can focus all our attention on a problem at hand until we solve it.

In this book we want to help you deal with some of our more troublesome emotions—anger, worry, depression, fear, and loneliness. We want you to gain victory over these emotions because they often keep us from being what we want to be, what God intended we should be. They also frustrate us and harm our relationships with others by building barriers around our lives that others can't scale, that we can't get around.

These troublesome emotions leave us feeling defeated. We desperately want to overcome them, but we've tried before and failed. Now we feel doomed to live with them for the rest of our lives. What can we do? I believe you can control any troublesome emotion by *changing your thinking* rather than your feelings. Most people think our emotions are our thoughts. When I feel sad, I think sad thoughts. When I feel depressed, I think depressed thoughts. But really the opposite happens. Your thoughts cause your emotions and behavior.

We think that something happens (a car pulls out in front of us, almost causing an accident) and then we respond with an emotion and/or behavior (anger—blowing the horn). But that's not really what happens. Rather, we encounter an event—*we think*—and then we feel and respond.

What Guides My Self-Talk?

Let's look at four basic assumptions that guide the way we talk to ourselves:

1. *Our thoughts create our emotions.* What do we mean by that? Let's imagine that as you walk out of the grocery store you're greeted at the door by a girl who says, "You sure are fat. Why don't you go on a diet?" How would you respond?

Right away you want more information. "How old is the girl?" Let's say she's four. You'll probably excuse her behavior as immature, hoping she'll outgrow it in the years to come. Let's change her age. She's fourteen. Now you probably get angry because even if what she says is true, it's not polite to talk that way. Let's add another fact. This fourteen-year-old is developmentally retarded, having the I.Q. of a five-year-old. Your anger disappears and is replaced with pity.

Our emotions, in each instance, are controlled by our

thinking rather than by the event itself. Our thoughts, then, do create our emotions!

2. *Our thoughts affect our behavior.* Shortly after Jimmy Hoffa disappeared, the *Detroit Free Press* carried an article on him that included this story: Once when Hoffa was being taken into court, a man suddenly stood, aimed a gun at him, and shouted, "Hoffa, you're dead."

How would you respond to such an attack? Some people would freeze in fear, saying to themselves, "I'm dead, there's nothing I can do." Others would say to themselves, "Unless I get under cover, I'm dead," and then dive for the nearest shelter. But not Hoffa. He charged the man and took away his gun. When asked later why he did it he said, "I figured that no one else would act, so I'd better." Hoffa's story is a good example of how our thoughts determine our actions.

3. *We tend to think irrationally.* While we might accept the other assumptions, this one hurts. Who wants to be considered irrational? "What an insult!" we think. We like to believe we are rational people, on top of things mentally and emotionally. And Christians in particular object because in a scientific world, they want to stake a claim to their carefully thought-out, rational religion. Let's check out what an age-old authority, the Bible, says.

Jeremiah, an Old Testament prophet, writes, "The heart is the most deceitful thing there is, and desperately wicked. No one can really know how bad it is!" (17:9). Today we would replace "heart" with "mind" (thoughts) because the Jews of that day believed that the heart was the source of all actions. Jeremiah tells us that our minds often deceive us. He also says our minds are deeply influenced by evil and suggests that only as we carefully observe our thinking can we avoid the irrationality that leads to sin.

David, a songwriter and fugitive, must also have realized this human problem. In Psalm 139:23-24 he prays, "Search me, O God, and know my heart; test my thoughts. Point out anything you find in me that makes you sad, and lead me along the path of everlasting life." Again a great man of God declares our thoughts suspect unless we frequently examine them and sort out the good from the bad.

What are some irrational thought patterns we fall into every day? Let's look at five common examples.

—*Overgeneralizing*. "Always" and "never" are words we use constantly. At home we hear things like, "You never come home on time." "You always burn the gravy." "You always leave your underwear on the bathroom floor." "You never do anything right." "You're never on time for a meeting." When we overgeneralize we often experience troublesome emotions as a result.

—*Emphasizing the negative side of our lives*. Perhaps you have heard two people talking about their diets say, "Last week when I went out for lunch with Dorothy I overate a little, like I usually do, but when the waitress came around and showed me a piece of banana cream pie topped with whipped cream, I just couldn't resist. I took it and blew my diet to pieces."

We may pass up 100 snacks in the course of a week, but when we get together with friends we talk about our one failure. When trying to control troublesome emotions we may experience victory 167½ out of 168 hours in a week, but as humans we tend to focus on the half hour of failure. To gain victory over our troublesome emotions we need to emphasize the positives, our successes, rather than our failures.

—*Jumping to conclusions*. When someone offends us we often tell ourselves, "If I tell them what I think, they'll get angry and they won't like me." How do we know they won't like us? *We just do*. Have we told them about things we didn't like in the past? Occasionally. Have they rejected us as a result? No. Then why won't they like us if we tell them now? Hmmm. They just won't. I just know they won't. We often act without evidence, jumping to conclusions before all the facts are in.

The Bible gives us a good example of this type of thinking. As the apostle Paul planned to leave on his second missionary trip, a young man named John Mark approached and asked, "Can I join you?" "Not on your life," responded Paul. "I don't want you to leave us again when we're halfway through." What a way to respond to an earnest young man! But Paul had taken John Mark on an earlier trip, and John Mark quit in the middle and went home, leaving Paul with all the work. Paul's partner, Barnabas, argued with him, but Paul refused to change his mind. He wouldn't take a man who deserted him once before.

But all the facts weren't in on John Mark. Yes, he failed miserably the first time, but now he had grown up. Barnabas recognized the new maturity and split from Paul, taking John Mark with him as a partner. And great things happened. Later Paul even asked John Mark to visit because he was such a valued friend.

—*Labeling people and behavior.* How many times have you heard, "Oh, she's just a dumb blonde!'"? Or, "Those teenagers! I just can't understand them!'"? Or, "I'm sick of being with old people. They're all the same"? The disciples were human like us. Once when Jesus was talking to a Samaritan woman—a half-breed—at a well (John 4), they were incredulous. They thought Jesus was wasting his time with a woman who couldn't possibly respond to the gospel. But she did.

When I was in seminary I worked as the junior high leader in a large suburban church. In October of my second year I was rushed to the hospital for an emergency appendectomy. Since I was already in misery, I didn't see any value in feeling worse by shaving, so I let my beard grow while I recovered. When it came time to go back to school and church I trimmed it, leaving what I felt was a nice goatee.

The week after I showed up again in church, my supervisor phoned me and told me that the church board had an ultimatum for me: "Either cut off your beard or quit working with the junior highers." I joked with him for a few moments and then replied, "I already cut it off because my wife didn't like it." But how sad that the church board had labeled me "not fit to work with church young people" just because I grew a beard. Whether Christians or non-Christians, all of us participate in some form of irrational thinking.

—*Assuming people are against us.* We've all had the experience of seeing two people talking with one another, occasionally glancing in our direction, laughing and joking back and forth, and had the uncomfortable feeling they were talking about us. One friend jokingly commented on this by saying, "I've quit attending football games. Each time a team huddles I wonder what they're saying about me." Our assumption that people are against us often results in emotions and behavior we don't like to find in ourselves.

4. *We tend to think in absolutes* like "I should . . ." "I shouldn't . . ." "I must . . ." "I have to . . ." or "I can't . . ."

Some absolutes can keep us in a state of turmoil if they lead us to impose impossible standards upon ourselves or make harmful false assumptions. Here are some familiar examples:

—"I have to get straight A's."
—"I can't succeed in my job without bending the rules."
—"I should volunteer to do more even though I am already overextended."
—"If only I had a new car I would be happy."

Thinking in absolutes such as these can burden us with negative, troublesome emotions and keep us from enjoying life.

Gaining Control
In these opening paragraphs we've seen that the things we say to ourselves as we live our lives really do affect our emotions. And consequently if we can learn to use self-talk in a positive way we can begin to transform our negative emotions into steps for growth. It's not easy—there's no magic wiggle-your-nose-and-you're-always-a-

positive-person formula, but we can learn to challenge our irrational self-talk with four questions:

1. *"Would an outside observer agree with my thinking?"* If I challenge myself by saying, "Is this true?" I'll respond with a quick "Yes" because I'm defensive about my own thinking. It's very difficult to be objective about yourself. But if you ask, "Would an outside observer agree with my thinking?" then you have to step outside yourself and look at the situation differently—through someone else's eyes.

Jon complained bitterly to his brother Scott, "You deliberately didn't send me an invitation to Eric's wedding, so we didn't come."

This is like the game of Clue. What really happened? An outside observer looking in might remember Scott, with obvious enthusiasm, telling Jon about the wedding a couple of weeks ago, assuming that he would be coming. But when Jon received no written invitation, he thought he was being snubbed. What happened to the invitation is still a mystery, but simply asking, "Would an outside observer agree with my thinking?" helped clear the air between Jon and Scott.

2. *"Is this thinking right and good for me?"* or does it make me feel bitter and bad about myself? This question often exposes negative thoughts as they are—thoughts that undermine our self-confidence and rot away our relationships with others.

If you are a Christian, you need to ask in addition, "Is this thinking Christian?" As Christians we need to consider not only how our thinking is affecting us but also how it affects others. By challenging our thoughts we control our irrational thinking by bringing it back under the control of Christ and his Word (2 Corinthians 10:5).

Elijah, a courageous Old Testament prophet, experienced a tremendous victory over the wicked Queen Jezebel and the cultic prophets of Baal, but when she told him he would die as soon as she got her hands on him, he turned and ran. When he at last stopped to rest he was so depressed and discouraged he asked God to take his life, complaining that he alone still served God and that no one else cared. God slowly brought him back into touch with reality by challenging his thinking with the ancient equivalent of, "Is this thinking Christian?" Elijah began again to see God's power for what it is.

3. *"How do I know this is true?"* As with many newlyweds, I didn't know how to respond to the differences of opinion my wife and I occasionally had. At first I thought when she did something I didn't like, "She's doing it deliberately, just to get me." Slowly a new thinking replaced those negative thoughts. "She did something I don't like, but I know if I talk with her about it she will try to do better the next time." My evaluation, "She deliberately seeks to hurt me," simply would not hold water.

Remember our tendency to assume people are against us. Each time we think this we need to challenge ourselves to bring out the evidence to support our thinking. The same is true with many other thoughts. Frequently when we try to display evidence to support our thoughts, whether good or bad, we discover there is none. This challenge also helps us control our irrational thoughts.

4. *"Would an alternative explanation fit the same facts?"* This question challenges us to look at all the angles.

Suppose someone said to you, "I can't believe you took off for the weekend again. You really should learn to be more responsible instead of being so spontaneous." You'd probably feel angry—at least until you have all the facts. Maybe the woman has two small children and resents the freedom you have.

As a marriage counselor, one of my tasks is helping couples fit the same facts into an alternative model. Elaine came for counseling, complaining that her husband Harold "has never held a permanent job the whole time we've been married. He's never worked for one company for more than two months without quitting. I've worked since the day we got married. Mine's the only regular income in our house."

Then Harold had his say. It even changed my thinking. Yes, he didn't like to work for other people, but that didn't mean that he was lazy. He related how he regularly rides the streets ahead of the garbage truck or cruises the countryside looking for junk he can salvage. He discovered that a lot of what other people call garbage he can turn into useful products again. He sees a discarded washing machine, gets permission to load it on his truck, takes it home and repairs it, trades it for something even better, works on that for a while, and then sells it for a profit.

When we actually got down to counting dollars, he brought home just as much as his wife. The problem lay in the fact that he never looked like he was working. He was just driving around town picking up junk or playing at fixing it up in his junk-filled acreage. It took a while, but eventually we put a different explanation on the facts and saw that a highly irregular lifestyle represented a man who worked hard and provided his family's needs, even though his wife originally saw it differently.

Each time we feel troublesome emotions gaining control we need to ask ourselves if an alternative explanation also could fit the facts.

Replacing the Bad with the Good
Now that we've examined why we think the way we do about ourselves, let's take a look at what we can do about negative self-talk. One way of overcoming our troublesome emotions is by replacing our bad thoughts with good ones. This may sound like nothing more than the power of positive thinking—it's not. But we do need to fill our minds with good thoughts if we want to live without troublesome emotions.

Our emotions *are* under our control. Most people find that a startling statement. We've lived so long with the popular psychology that tells us our emotions are beyond our control, that we've lost all other perspectives. The Bible argues that we can control our emotions by consciously choosing to think about good things. For example, Paul tells us, "Fix your thoughts on what is true and good and right. Think about things that are pure and lovely, and dwell on the fine, good things in others" (Philippians 4:8).

Even before you start, however, I can guarantee problems. You'll fail occasionally while you're trying to change. But what's wrong with that? It doesn't make *you* a failure. In fact, occasional failure is part of learning any new behavior.

A few years ago I took Mike out cross-country skiing

with me. He'd never been out before and he fell frequently. While he's a good athlete, this was something new, and I could see that he was getting discouraged.

After a while I stopped and said, "You know, Mike, falling down is part of learning how to ski. You simply keep getting up until at last you come to the point where you rarely fall." I noticed a brightening in his attitude, and that's just what happened. The more he tried, the fewer times he fell until he developed into a good skier. We need to learn to see occasional failure as part of the process of learning how to change.

What does that mean? It means we need to give ourselves the freedom to fail *while changing*. It means we shouldn't berate ourselves for eating one chocolate chip cookie when we have rigorously stuck to a diet for three months, and we shouldn't flail ourselves if we yell at our husband or wife for the first time in months when we used to fight every day. Many Christians have a hard time with failing because these troublesome emotions we're talking about are sometimes also sin. Can I really give myself the freedom to sin while trying to gain control over my emotions? I think so.

The Holy Spirit presents us with a mystery in the New Testament. He holds before us the ideal of perfection. Jesus even says on one occasion, "But you are to be perfect, even as your Father in heaven is perfect" (Matthew 5:48). On the other hand he makes provision for each time we fail. In 1 John 1:9 he tells us, "If we confess our sins to him, he can be depended on to forgive us and to cleanse us from every wrong."

Thus God issues both a call to perfection and a promise

to redeem us in our failures. This means God himself is saying, "I know you'll fail while trying to change. Don't worry about it. Each time you fail, just admit it to me, and I'll pick you up and get you started again. Eventually the time will come when you'll quit falling down. Until then I'm ready and willing to help you back on your feet each time you fall."

This is similar to good child discipline. When children fail to distinguish right from wrong we both correct them and help them get back on track again. We recognize that moral maturity is in part tied to developing physical, mental, and psychological maturity. While their failures need correction, they also evoke love and concern from us as we seek to restore them. God treats us the same way, encouraging us to focus on the good things happening in our lives rather than on our failures.

Psychology Today recently reported on the power of thought to change our behavior. Three groups were tested on their ability to make free throws with a basketball. After the initial testing the first group was told not to touch a basketball for the next week until they were tested again. The second group was told to practice for an hour each day. The third group was told to *think* about successful free throws for an hour each day. At the end of the week each group was re-tested.

The group that didn't practice didn't improve—just as expected. The group that practiced an hour daily improved significantly. The group that merely thought about successfully shooting free throws, however, improved almost as much as the group that practiced an hour daily. If you can simply dream about victory over your troublesome emotions by focusing on your successes, you'll go a long way toward changing. Your thoughts have power!

In addition, visualize the benefits that would come into your life through this type of success. Imagine the changes in your relationships with others, in your feelings about yourself. Imagine the things you could do that you can't now. This will also help you gain control.

Learn to challenge your excuses for failing. A few weeks ago I stood in the checkout line at the grocery store when a woman suddenly rushed up and exclaimed, "Oh, I'm late for my beauty appointment." With that she rushed to the head of the line, plopped down her few items with a twenty-dollar bill, and stood waiting to be checked out. No one complained or told her to go back to where she belonged. Why? Because she gave an excuse to justify her inexcusable behavior. None of us believed her excuse justified what she did. But by giving an excuse she gave just enough reason for us to let her do what we all knew was wrong.

Similarly our troublesome emotions are all supported by excuses that are no more substantial than hers, but we keep giving them because they permit us to do what we know is wrong. We regularly justify our troublesome emotions with excuses we *don't believe*. How can we stop?

We need to develop counter-thought. A counter-thought is a challenge to our excuse that says, "That's not right." Developing counter-thoughts is usually easy because most of us know our excuses don't hold water, even though we've used them for years and become comfortable with them. A few moments' thought is usually enough to create three or four counter-thoughts to challenge each excuse.

I used to bite my fingernails until they bled. No matter how much it hurt I could always justify nibbling further by telling myself, "But you're just straightening out a rough spot." And I was—even if I had created it by earlier biting. I would then bite until I could bite no more. Now I solve the problem by telling myself to get out a nail file and smooth them properly. It destroys my excuse and keeps me from biting my nails.

Finally, we need to consciously focus our thoughts on what is good, just as Paul says in Philippians 4:8. Each time we discover a negative thought in our minds, we need to consciously replace it with a positive one. This is important because you can't *not* think about anything. You can't not be angry, depressed, lonely, worried, or any other negative emotion. But what you can do is consciously focus on something positive as a means of shoving these negative thoughts from your mind.

Learn to develop God's perspectives on life. Seek him out as a conversation partner. Pick up the dusty Bible from your shelf and open it up. God can become your companion as you read and study, and he'll teach you how to talk with him in prayer. You'll be surprised at the Bible's wealth of material and knowledge that applies to your problem area. Memorizing Scripture to hold off negative thoughts will give you a stronghold when you feel your world and emotions crumbling around you.

My friend Jeff and I were excited as we started skiing into the Hoist Lake area. We'd waited all winter for a good snow and free time to be able to cross-country ski together. We planned on skiing six miles into the wilderness of northern Michigan and then six miles back. About a mile from the car, Jeff's ski broke. He could very easily have complained bitterly about his luck. We'd planned this trip for months and had driven about fifty miles to get there. Now his day was finished. As he looked at his ski he said, "Isn't it nice it broke here instead of way out on the trail?" Similarly we need to be able to look at the worst event and respond to it by seeking the good in the worst.

As you learn to control your thinking, you'll slowly gain control of your emotions as well. Then you'll begin to enjoy a freedom you never imagined possible. Slowly you'll come to control your emotions rather than letting them control you. I urge you to begin today to change your thinking as a means of changing your emotions. Challenge your negative self-talk with the questions we suggested. And focus on exchanging your bad thoughts for good ones.

Things to Do/Think About:
1. Recall a troublesome emotion from this past week. Write out a brief statement of your thoughts at the time.
2. Apply the four challenge questions for negative self-talk to your own self-talk. What do you discover?
3. Examine the three means of replacing bad thoughts with good ones. How can you use them this week?
4. Which of the five common irrational thought patterns applies to your thinking? Why?
5. Each time you experience a troublesome emotion, examine your self-talk to see how you created it. You might learn something new about yourself in the process!

For Further Reading:
Jerry Schmidt, *Do You Hear What You're Thinking* (Victor Books)
David Stoop, *Self-Talk* (Revell)

2

I Never Worry (Do I?)

I STOOD WATCHING THE MECHANIC work on my car with a growing sense of foreboding. While it wasn't a new car by any means, I had just purchased it four days ago. Now it had overheated and warped the plate holding the thermostat. I grabbed the owner's manual and placed a call I should have made before I bought the car. When I talked with the previous owner I learned that the used car dealer had set my speedometer back almost 50,000 miles.

I was furious and deeply worried. As a graduate student and part-time pastor with a son barely a year old, I had put everything I could into that car. Now it was far older than I had imagined. I couldn't concentrate on anything else. Each time I thought about the car, the need to talk with the dealer, and my financial position, my mind took off on a disaster trek, imagining all the things that could go wrong. The time until I could speak with the dealer was agony. All that agony for nothing! When I finally talked with the dealer, he quickly refunded my money and apologized (I'm sure he was afraid of a lawsuit). But worry sure played havoc with me for a time.

Worrying is probably the least effective approach to a problem. We know this. Nevertheless we still choose to worry rather than to act.

What does worry do? It actually prevents problem solving. It gives us something to do about the problem that actually sidetracks us from effectively solving it.

Worry Is . . .

What is worry? What's the difference between worry, anxiety, and concern? Aren't they the same? Let's take a look.

Anxiety is the normal tension we experience when we try to do well. The student with cold, clammy hands just before an important exam is experiencing anxiety. So is the newly-married wife preparing dinner for her in-laws for the first time, or the businessman pacing the floor just before his big presentation before the board.

Each Sunday morning when I enter the pulpit, I'm anxious. It's not that I'm afraid I will make a fool of myself or fail, although occasionally when I leave the pulpit I'm not happy with the way things went. It's simply that I want to do a good job in serving God and his people. This results in a number of minor problems each week. I hardly ever sleep well Saturday night, and I'm usually mildly constipated Sunday morning. All this is the result of a normal, perfectly acceptable level of anxiety about doing a good job.

Worry is also different from concern. Concern is recognizing and facing potential problems—but with confidence in God and yourself and hope for the future. Job, an Old Testament father, illustrates this. The Bible calls him a righteous man, perfect in God's sight (Job 1:1). Yet each day Job made sacrifices to God for whatever sins his children might have inadvertently committed during the day. He knew they might sin and did everything he could to take care of it. But when his children were killed, his animals were destroyed, and he himself was dreadfully ill, he still committed himself to God without complaint. He was legitimately concerned while completely trusting God.

Worry is negative, useless, aggravating self-talk. It's a conversation with ourselves that accomplishes nothing other than to disturb us more. It is aggravating because it complicates the problems we face by arousing our emotions without proposing any solutions. It is negative because it highlights everything bad about the problem while failing to deal with the good or any potential solutions.

Anxiety and concern are legitimate approaches to various problems in life. But worry is a choice to stew about a problem rather than to deal constructively with it.

Worry, however, often does not even deal with real problems. It often deals with negative events (past or potential) that you cannot do anything about. You may worry about the past you cannot change. You may worry about Uncle Larry's negative response to your joking comment, about sister Sue's anger when you commented on her first gray hair, about the sins in your past that cannot be changed. If you carefully examine your worries, you may discover that many are about past events that cannot be changed simply because *they are past*.

We also worry about future events we cannot do anything about. We worry about possible illness. Will we get cancer? Will the children get the flu? Will my husband have to miss work this winter because of illness? Will he lose his job in the economic fluctuations? Will it rain on the day of the big ball game?

But what can we do about these things? They are largely beyond our control. There is little we can do to stop them from happening. Then why worry about them? It seems rather foolish. We need only wait until they do (or more often *do not*) happen and then deal with them.

We also frequently worry about trivial things that don't really matter in the long run. What difference will it make if you are not perfectly dressed, if a hair is out of place, if a neighbor finds dust in your house, if you are five minutes late for an appointment, if it rains on a picnic, if you have a flat tire, if one of the children gets a cold?

The Bible gives us another good example of such misplaced worry in a story about two sisters, Mary and Martha. When Jesus came to visit (Luke 10:38-42), Martha hurried about the house making certain everything was perfect for Jesus' dinner while Mary sat quietly at his feet in the living room listening to his remarkable wisdom. Eventually when Martha exploded in anger at her sister's negligence, Jesus helped her see that his words were far more important in the long run than what he ate or a beautiful setting.

Some people worry about other people's problems. That may sound strange, but as a counselor I find this is one of the biggest problems many families face. Shirley complains, "I just can't get my husband up in time for work. I call him over and over; sometimes I physically drag him out of bed. I constantly push him about getting dressed, eating, shaving, and getting out the door in time to get to work."

But his getting to work on time is not really her problem. If he shows up late for work, who is the boss going to yell at? Will he call her at home and ask, "Why are you failing as a wife? Don't you know you're responsible to get your husband to work on time?" Not likely. He'll bawl her husband out and warn him he'll be fired unless he shapes up.

Parents act the same way. They worry about their children's homework, about their getting to school on time, about their getting too warm, too cold, about their doing the jobs they've accepted in the neighborhood. Spouses worry about one another's job responsibilities, household chores, meeting appointments. Children worry about their parents' ability to handle money and responsibility as they get older, about their driving skills. We frequently chide our children when they assume responsibility for their siblings, "When you have all your own problems solved, then you can take responsibility for your brother's problems." We need to remember this as adults in our relationships with others.

Finally, we worry about the future we can change. This is the only legitimate worry we have, but even that should not be a worry. As soon as we realize we are worrying about something we can change, we should make a plan to change it. Worry is useless, but planning and acting get things done.

Our worrying reveals a basic lack of trust in God as our loving heavenly Father. The Bible tells us, "Since he did not spare even his own Son for us but gave him up for us all, won't he also surely give us everything else?" (Romans 8:32). God plans to give his children all the good he thinks they can handle. He allowed his own son to die in agony on a cross so that each one of us could be saved from eternal punishment, if only we choose.

But when we worry we tell God, "God, you can't cut it without my help. Give me a few days to worry about this problem and then you and I can really do a bang-up job of solving it. But if you don't give me the time to worry about it, then I'm sure you'll fail." While none of us would put it that bluntly, that is precisely what we tell God by our actions when we worry.

Worry Creates Problems

Worry messes up our lives in so many different ways that there should be significant cause for us to abandon it.

Ulcers, high blood pressure, various intestinal disorders, allergies, and many cardiovascular problems are caused in part or are aggravated by worry. Regular constipation, diarrhea, and colitis are frequently signs of worry. Many allergies are related to our worrying about problems rather than dealing with them.

Worry also causes social problems. When we worry we alienate others by becoming so preoccupied with our problems we have no time for theirs. After a while, our friends and family tire of hearing our complaints, particularly when they know we aren't actually doing anything about them. Soon people avoid us because they don't want us to rehearse our latest worry.

One friend told me this story: His office had been having problems with their furnace for months. He'd asked Arnie, the maintenance man, to call the plumber. Weeks passed. Nothing happened. So finally he phoned the plumber himself to find out the reason for the long delay in getting the furnace fixed.

The plumber commented, "Yes, Arnie did call. But to be frank, I didn't want to call him back and talk with him. Once he gets on the phone I have to listen to him complain forever about what's going on in his life. So I keep putting it off, and putting it off, delaying the work I should be doing." Arnie's worries were the source of many not-too-funny jokes around the office.

Finally, worry creates spiritual problems by separating us from God. At its root, worry is a lack of trust in God's ability to deal with our problems. When we worry we tell God, "I really don't trust you to care for me," and we withdraw from him. We must remember one thing: worry and trust are incompatible.

Creating a Solution

What is the solution, then, to worry? We need a solution that does three things for us. First, it eliminates false issues so that we have time and energy to deal with the real issues. Second, it enables us to deal with the real issues. And finally, it should be founded in God's eternal character.

1. *We need to eliminate false issues.* How do we do that? Here are three suggestions that can work together or separately. First, challenge yourself with self-talk questions about your worrying. Ask, *"Is there really anything I can do about this problem?"* Since much of our worrying is about things we can't control, we need to challenge ourselves by asking if there really is anything we *can* do about it.

I've found that I get my work done best when I establish daily, weekly, and monthly goals. But goals are targets, and sometimes during the course of a day I experience so many interruptions I simply cannot meet my goals for the day. When this happens I talk to myself. "Remember, goals are not cast in concrete. You can do the work another day." And finally, "You can do nothing about the interruptions since that is just part of life." I find that when I talk to myself like this, I can relax and do as much as possible without being frustrated about interruptions.

The second question we need to ask ourselves relates to trivia. But we need to be careful how we phrase it. If I ask you, "Is what you're worrying about trivial?" you would respond, "No." None of us likes to think our worries are trivial. We can change our perspective on this question by posing it like this: *"If someone else were asked to evaluate your worry, would he consider it trivial?"* From that perspective, we often have to say, "Yes." Others would judge our worry as trivial. If so, then we need to put it aside.

The third question is, *"Am I taking on someone else's responsibility?"* The housewife who dragged her husband out of bed and pushed him to work is a good example of this. The Bible gives us another colorful example in Abraham, who flees the land of Canaan to go to Egypt during a time of famine (Genesis 12:10-20). As he travels to Egypt with his wife, Sarah, he begins to worry about the Egyptian leader Pharaoh's response once they arrive. What if Pharaoh finds Sarah so attractive that he wants her as part of his harem? Since she is Abraham's wife, Pharaoh might kill Abraham to free her to marry him.

Eventually Abraham tells Sarah to lie to Pharaoh and say that she is only his sister. Why? Because he is afraid and wants to save his own skin. But protecting Abraham is not Abraham's responsibility—it is God's. And when he began his journey, he knew he must go down to Egypt or face starvation. God promised to care for him and guide him. He promised Abraham a wonderful future. And yet Abraham gets himself into trouble by assuming God's responsibility for his care. Abraham was human— just like us.

Money forces most Christians to face this issue. If I'm honestly seeking to handle money in a Christian manner, when I face an unexpected bill, what should I do? Many people worry, but that's wrong. God is responsible to take care of the legitimate needs of his children. When I attended college and faced bills without money, I learned to pray, "Well, God, you've called me to college. That means I need money. I've been responsible in my finances. I don't have enough right now and some bills are coming up. What are you going to do about it?" I then left it in his hands, and he never blew it. Those bills were his responsibility, and he was faithful.

After you've asked yourself these questions, you need to talk to yourself about what you discover. Tell yourself not to worry about things you can't control. Tell yourself that in the long run, your worry is trivial. Tell yourself that this is someone else's responsibility, so you don't have to worry about it. This may sound like an easy answer to the problem of worry, but it's not. It takes a lot of work and motivation on your part. Don't worry! You can do it. Keep telling yourself these things until at last you're able to lay your worry aside.

Sometimes that doesn't work. Sometimes our worries are like a circular tape reel that keeps playing the same message over and over. We honestly wonder if we will ever break free. When that happens we need a more powerful solution—prayer. And what is prayer? A way of communicating directly with our Creator who knows all about us, his created. He knows about our joys, our sadnesses, our sordid pasts. And we can call on him directly to protect us against the evil that Satan wants to work in us. And as we pray and learn more about the Bible, we can use the technique that Jesus does in Matthew 4:1-11 when Satan tempts him in the wilderness.

Each time Satan tempted Jesus he responded with the same basic speech pattern. "The Bible says . . ." When we face an obsessive worry, we can also use God's Word to rebuke Satan directly. But we need to use the utmost caution here: Jesus was a man, but he was also God. And since we are only human, we must include in our rebuke the name of Jesus, who conquered Satan at Calvary through his death and resurrection. Satan is already defeated—Jesus put a strangling hold on him at the Cross. We need only claim his victory.

When our worry becomes obsessive, we then respond to Satan by saying, "Satan, in the name of Jesus Christ, I command you to leave me alone, for the Bible says, 'Don't worry about anything; instead, pray about everything; tell God your needs' " (Philippians 4:6). And you will be surprised how fast evil retreats in the face of Scripture—there is nothing Satan hates more than hearing the Word of God.

We can speak directly to Satan because he is just as much a person as God, the angels, and we are. We use the Bible because it's the only offensive weapon God gave us. And we speak in Jesus' name because if we are Christians, we are his and have power over Satan through his death and resurrection. When we respond in this way, success is often amazingly quick and easy. If we do not choose Christ as the ruler and guide of our minds and hearts, we leave ourselves open as easy prey for Satan, the destroyer.

2. *We need to deal with the real issues.* Sometimes our worries deal with real issues, issues that are our responsibility, that are not trivial, and that we can affect. When that's the case we need to create a "to-do" list—things we want to do in the future. For example, if we're worried about our children's education, we should plan to begin a college fund for them; or if we're concerned about a home for our family, we should work out a budget to save up to buy a house.

The Bible again provides a good example in Jacob, a

young trickster who slowly grew to maturity after causing all sorts of problems in his family. When he first meets his brother Esau after twenty years of exile (Genesis 32-33), he sends ahead gifts to appease his brother's anger at his trickery. When these apparently do not work, he makes a plan. He divides his company so those least important to him are in front and those most important are protected in the back. He then withdraws to pray. The next day when he meets his brother, he handles a delicate situation with care.

When we begin to worry about some situation where we can act, we should write down that worry and then plan what we can do—taking into account every possibility.

3. *We need to base the solution on God's eternal character.* Finally, throughout all of this, we need to base the solution on God's character as our heavenly Father who loves us and always seeks our best. In Romans 8:32 Paul says that after God gave up his son to die for us on the cross, how could we imagine that he would withhold anything good from us? We place our worries in perspective by reminding ourselves that our loving heavenly Father wants and does what is best for us.

He not only wants what is best, but also knows what is best. As parents we want what is best for our children. Sometimes, however, we don't learn what is really best until we've already acted, sometimes not until our children are gone and there is nothing more we can do about it. But God is an all-knowing heavenly parent. He knows what is best for us in addition to desiring it. This is why the author of Proverbs says, ". . . trust in the Lord completely; don't ever trust yourself. In everything you do, put God first, and he will direct you and crown your efforts with success" (3:5-6). As we trust God our worries diminish.

We also recognize that our heavenly Father is a sovereign God. Therefore *he always accomplishes what is best for us.* In Romans 8:28 Paul tells us, "And we know that God causes all things to work together for good to those who love God, to those who are called according to His purpose" (NASB). No matter what we face, the Holy Spirit is in the midst of the situation, working to create something valuable for those who love him, for those whom he has called. God wants what is best for us, knows what is best for us, and has the power to accomplish what is best for us.

A New Kind of Freedom

What's the result of following the suggestions for freedom from worry? Peace with ourselves, peace with others, and peace with God.

Peace with ourselves means that we can lie down at night and go to sleep without our minds racing over our worries. It means we can live with acceptable levels of anxiety in the situations we face each day. It means that physical problems we create with worry disappear. (It sure is nice to be rid of the ulcers I had when I worried too much!)

We are also at peace with others. No longer do we upset or bore them with our regular litany of worries. We no longer approach each encounter with another person wondering if they are going to like us, or get angry with us. We can move through life with confidence.

Finally, we are at peace with God. We know that no matter what we face in life he walks with us. His love enables us to face anything. His power assures us we will ultimately be successful. And we can rejoice in what he is making us.

How can we gain this peace? Through positive, constructive self-talk. Whenever we begin to worry, we need to talk to ourselves using the principles we've laid out in these two chapters. Since worry is negative, aggravating self-talk, we only gain victory over it when we replace it with positive, calming self-talk.

Things to Do/Think About:

1. Recall a recent situation where you worried. Ask yourself the three questions that challenge worry and apply them to your particular situation (see *Creating a Solution*, #1).

2. Write down how the three character traits of God which overcome worry apply to that situation (see *Creating a Solution*, #3).

3

I Am NOT Angry!

SHORTLY AFTER GERI AND I GOT MARRIED we bought our first and only brand new car, a Volkswagon hatchback. We were both proud and naive in our new possession. Each time I found something wrong with the car, since it was under warranty, I trotted it back to the dealer for repairs. Each time I picked the car up, I discovered that while fixing one thing, the dealer had messed up another. I patiently returned, explained how I wished he would get everything right the first time, and waited for results. They never came.

Finally I told Geri just before leaving for the garage and the latest repair work, "I'm going to make a scene today. I'm going to shout and scream right in the middle of his showroom about his lousy service."

I did just that. I don't ever remember them making another mistake while fixing my car, and they gave me the red-carpet treatment each time I stepped into the dealership. But I didn't like what I had to do to get that sort of service.

This is often the way we feel when we make a scene. We know it works, but we don't like doing it. We are embarrassed, we feel guilty. Often we leave feeling remorseful at what we did, but then we brag to friends and relatives about how we put someone in his/her place. We are curiously ambivalent about our anger.

We are of two minds. We get angry. None of us denies that we get angry. But nevertheless we think anger is wrong. We imagine ourselves a rational people, and anger is emotional, not rational.

Christians in particular struggle with this because we're convinced the Bible says anger is wrong. Nonetheless we're bombarded by popular columnists, radio teachers, books, and magazine articles telling us to "let it all hang out," and urging us not to be a doormat. Either you get angry or you pay the price. And what happens if you keep it all inside? Your anger will create psychological problems. You'll explode. All this unless you let your anger out.

God Gets Angry
Surprised? Let's look at what the Bible says about anger. We begin by noting that God *does* get angry. Many people have a hard time with that. When we see anger we focus on its evil, destructive side. We can't imagine how God can get angry without doing wrong. Yet the Bible shows again and again that God gets angry.

In Psalm 78:30-31 the psalmist relates Israel's history in poetry, recalling their wilderness experience of prolonged wandering. They ate manna day in and day out for forty years. Once they complained to God about their diet. They were tired of eating bread every day, for every meal, with no relief in sight. Quite a dull menu! Even the greatest of chefs could not have come up with a new way to prepare manna after so long. They wanted meat like they had back in Egypt. They seemed to forget that they had been slaves in Egypt and that God had rescued them. After they complained long enough, God gave them meat—but while they were still eating it he also punished them for their ungrateful complaining. Many of them died as a result of his anger.

The classic biblical statement on God's anger is Romans 1:18: "But God shows his anger from heaven against all sinful, evil men who push away the truth from them." God gets angry with all sin and unrighteousness. Because earlier versions of the Bible used the older word, *wrath,* we often miss the force of this passage. It's easy to read about God's wrath at sin without seeing the full force of what Paul says. He says God gets angry with all sin and all unrighteousness. No one escapes his anger.

Maybe we can accept anger in God more readily, however, if we look at anger in Jesus' life. Jesus is not only fully God, he is also fully human. He never sinned during his lifetime (Hebrews 4:15), yet on at least one occasion, the Bible clearly states that Jesus was angry.

One Sabbath day, Jesus stopped in the local synagogue to worship and teach. He entered a synagogue full of people anticipating his arrival, none more excited about his coming than the religious leaders. Not that they welcomed his visit. They knew a man with a withered hand was also there, and they wanted to see if Jesus would heal the man on the Sabbath, the day of rest and consecration to God. Their interpretation of the Old Testament code said healing on the Sabbath was wrong if the healing could be postponed for another day.

When Jesus saw the man and sensed the religious leaders' attitude, he challenged them with a question. "Is it right to do good on the Sabbath day, or to do harm? To save life, or to destroy it?" (Luke 6:9).

But they silently stood watching for his response. The Bible then records, "He looked around them one by one and then said to the man, 'Reach out your hand.' And as he did, it became completely normal again" (Luke 6:10). He was angry, however, with the religious leaders because they were more concerned with their laws than with a man's healing.

On two occasions during his ministry Jesus cleansed the temple of money-changers (John 2:14-17). While the Bible does not directly say he was angry, it's difficult to understand these passages without assuming he was. He chased the money-changers from the temple with a whip of cords. Their response shows he was a man filled with anger. No cold calculated whipping would have caused the whole group to flee or disrupted their businesses so thoroughly.

Anger Is All Right—Sometimes

That God can get angry suggests that we also can get angry without sin. Anger then is all right for us—sometimes. If we use these two illustrations of Jesus' anger we can understand when and how anger can be right for us.

We can rightfully be angry at sin. The money-changers were "legally" cheating people. They also conducted business in the only place where the Gentiles were permitted to worship. Once a year every Jewish male had to pay a temple tax to support the temple and priesthood. Since Roman coins bore the emperor's image and many Romans worshiped him as a god, the religious leaders would not accept Roman money for the temple tax. Instead they minted their own coins.

This meant worshipers had to exchange Roman currency for the temple coins in order to pay their taxes. The money-changers, however, charged an exorbitant exchange rate. They literally stole from people who were trying to worship God. Jesus was angered by their sinful behavior, suggesting we also can be angry with sin. The sins of divorce, flagrant immorality, abortion on demand, and many others could be listed. There are many sins in our world that not only permit us to be angry but demand our rightful anger.

We are also justified in getting angry at the injustice and oppression of others. When Jesus healed a man's withered hand he was also struck by the way the religious leaders had oppressed the man. As with many wealthy people who write laws, they had no comprehension of the suffering their rules made for poor people. It was easy for them to say there should be no healing on the Sabbath because their wealth made it easy for them to get a physician any time they needed help. But the poor man was required to work six (sometimes seven) days a week. The only time he had free was the Sabbath. Struck by the oppressiveness of the religious leaders' rules, Jesus was rightfully angry.

We too can rightfully be angry when we see others treated unjustly. Much of what we call civil rights abuse falls under this category. The growing problem of abuse in families meets this criterion. When we see the abuse, both mental and physical, that some people experience in their families, we *should* get angry. It's wrong for people to be so oppressed by others.

The Wrong Kind of Anger

Having shown that anger is right—sometimes—we now need to emphasize that this is not the dominant theme in the Bible. Most of the time the Bible says anger is wrong, and for many reasons.

Our reasons for anger are often too small. Solomon writes in Proverbs 19:11, "A wise man restrains his anger and overlooks insults. This is to his credit." The wise man is one who can take an offense without getting angry. He doesn't have to retaliate each time someone crosses him. But our anger is often for small reasons. To put it bluntly, *we are selfish.* By our anger we demand that others conform to our expectations. When they fail, we punish them by getting angry.

A second reason why our anger is often wrong is that *we overreact.* Paul tells us that love is not irritable (1 Corinthians 13:5), but we have to admit that we often respond all out of proportion to the things that upset us. A child breaks a plate and a parent responds in rage. A husband leaves his shirt crumpled on the closet floor, and his wife blows her stack. A wife puts a small dent in the car and her husband explodes. We over-respond to what happens. We simply get too angry.

Third, when we get rightfully angry, *we stay angry too long*. Paul warns in Ephesians 4:26, "If you are angry, don't sin by nursing your grudge. Don't let the sun go down with you still angry—get over it quickly; for when you are angry you give a mighty foothold to the devil." But we often wallow in our hurt, enjoying every minute of it. We particularly enjoy the opportunity it gives us to gossip about others as we tell how they hurt us. The tragedy of this is that we slowly develop a bitter spirit—the opposite of the spirit of love the Bible calls for.

In the Old Testament account, Absalom felt deeply hurt. His stepbrother had raped his sister. When Absalom exacted primitive justice by killing the offending brother, their father, King David, banished Absalom from the kingdom. Eventually, however, David saw his error and permitted his son to return—but he refused to meet with him personally. Absalom allowed this rebuke to eat at him day by day for years until finally he attacked his father and grabbed the throne for himself. When David tried to recover the throne, Absalom was killed. None of it would have happened if Absalom would have given up his anger. By nursing his anger beyond what was reasonable, he eventually lost his life.

Fourth, when we get angry, *we get angry too quickly*. James warns us, be "slow to anger" (James 1:19, NASB). We should not be known for a quick temper, because unjustified anger does not accomplish God's goals for our lives. My guess is that most of the time when we get angry with family members, we get angry before we fully understand the situation. We get angry on insufficient evidence. If only we sought to understand all the facts before we responded, we would not get angry.

Annette heard the crash of breaking dishes. Dropping what she was doing, she rushed to the kitchen to find three of her new plates, anniversary presents, lying in pieces on the floor. Her four-year-old son, Tommy, stood on a chair, fear etching his face and tears beginning to roll from his eyes. "Haven't I told you to leave my dishes alone? Haven't I told you not to climb on chairs to get into the cabinets?" his mother yelled. She grabbed her son, smacked his bottom, sent him to his room, and began to clean up the mess.

Later when she calmed down, she went to his room to see how he was doing. He lay on his bed, quietly sobbing into his pillow. As she sat down beside him, he whimpered, "I was trying to put your new dishes away so you wouldn't have to work so hard."

How often we get angry before all the evidence is in!

Fifth, *we get angry with people rather than with sin and its effects*. When we have close relationships with others, we occasionally get angry with them. The closer we get, the more opportunities there are for frustration—one of the foundations for anger. Yet conflicts in relationships are natural.

If we closely examine the situation, we will probably discover that the real problem is *our* reaction, not the other person's action. Other people in the same situation might readily tolerate the behavior that angers us. I've noticed that I often respond in anger when someone tries to talk down to me. Yet I've noticed that others in the same situation can be quite accepting. The problem is not that some people talk down to others, but that some people can't stand having others talk down to them. Much of the time conflict can be handled by focusing on our response rather than seeking to discover who's to blame.

When we lay blame, we seem to focus more on revenge than on problem solving. Sometimes we enjoy thinking of the different ways we could hurt the other person rather than thinking of solutions to the problem. It's not that we actually plan to *do* anything, but it's enjoyable to think of all we *might* do. And through seeking revenge, our anger leads us into sin.

Anger also opens the door to temptation. Paul warns of this in Ephesians 4:27 when he says, "When you are angry you give a mighty foothold to the devil." When we are angry, we are more open to sin than at other times in our lives.

Angie's mom and dad had just split up after seventeen years of marriage. She was angry. For years they'd preached to her about living the Christian life and doing what the Bible says. On more than one occasion they'd sharply criticized those who divorced. Now they were separating. Angie decided to show them they weren't the only ones who could throw over the old rules. Her lifestyle changed radically. It wasn't too long until she was pregnant. Her anger opened her to behavior she would have rejected a few months earlier and blinded her to sin until it was too late. A stark example—but all of us do the same thing to different degrees.

Most significantly, anger keeps the Holy Spirit from working through us. When James warns us to be slow to get angry, he tells us our anger does not accomplish God's will (1:19-20). In the larger context of the biblical teaching on anger, we know that sometimes anger can accomplish God's purpose. But as a general rule our anger prevents the Holy Spirit from working through us, often with tragic results.

A Biblical Response to Anger

What then is a biblical response to the provocations that lead to anger? *First, we should forgive those who hurt us.* This certainly isn't easy, but God instructs us to exhibit this behavior in Ephesians 4:32. Each of us is responsible for the death of God's son, Jesus, on the cross. Yet God reaches out and offers us forgiveness if only we will take what he offers. No hurt we experience can ever compare with the pain God felt when his son died for our sins, yet he offers each of us forgiveness for our part in Jesus' death. What a loving, forgiving father God is!

We should also forgive others for the sins they have committed against us, instead of responding in anger to our hurt. Not only does God show us how to forgive, he also instructs, "Never avenge yourselves. Leave that to God, for he has said that he will repay those who deserve it" (Romans 12:19). Vengeance is never our responsibility, but how we love to take it upon ourselves! When we've been hurt our response should be to forgive, leaving vengeance in God's hands. He alone really knows what happened and just how much punishment our offender deserves.

Our second response should be patience. When someone

slanders us, we should be patient. We can do this because God showed tremendous patience in his dealings with us. He has not given us what we deserve. And even though we have often sinned he calls us to repentance again and again (2 Peter 3:9). He calls us to respond in like manner in our dealings with others.

He calls us to respond with patience because he creates good out of any situation we face. This is the meaning of Romans 8:28. No matter what happens to us, there in the midst of our hurt, God is working to create something of value out of our experience. By his great power and because of his great love he creates good out of all the bad things and circumstances that enter our lives. In response we can patiently wait for him to work his purpose.

Finally, we should be joyful in times of adversity. As God's children we know that God withholds nothing good from us. When God has already offered his son for our sins, can we really imagine he will now withhold anything good from us? Not on your life! Thus when others provoke us, we need to focus on the blessings in our lives.

Think about all you can praise God for and be glad about. As you do this, you will be able to respond to God with joy even when you face severe hardship.

When We Fail

We don't always respond as God wants. Sometimes we respond in anger. What are we to do then? First, we must deal with it quickly, if possible even before going to sleep tonight. Paul advises us in Ephesians 4:26 to deal with all our anger on the same day it occurs, never leaving any anger for the next day.

We should also take care of our anger before we approach God in worship. While Matthew 5:23-24 is not specifically about anger, it talks about sin and an injured friend. Jesus says, "So if you are standing before the altar in the Temple, offering a sacrifice to God, and suddenly remember that a friend has something against you, leave your sacrifice there beside the altar and go and apologize and be reconciled to him, and then come and offer your sacrifice to God." This suggests that we should even lay aside our plans for worship until we have dealt with the anger in our lives.

There's a reason for this. When you resolve your anger with a Christian friend, you restore fellowship and prevent that person from falling away from God. And doing that, Jesus says, "you have won back a brother" (Matthew 18:15).

But how do we apply all of this? I know that if I'd just finished reading this chapter, I would be frustrated. Intellectually, I know I need to respond to anger with patience. I know I should face the trials of life with joy. But how can I do it with all my heart? How can I control my all-too-human emotions? We'll look at this problem more closely in the next chapter.

Things to Do/Think About:
1. You are facing a situation that is highly frustrating and you sense that you are losing control. Write out self-talk that will give you biblical support in controlling your anger.
2. Think of a time when you were angry recently. Write out the reasons why it was either sinful or justifiable. Or both.

For Further Reading:
H. Norman Wright, *Dealing with Frustration and Anger* (Harvest House)
Lewis Smedes, *Forgive and Forget* (Harper and Row)

4

Putting a Bridle on Anger

Anger is a ferocious tiger caged inside each of us.
It stalks, waiting for an opportune moment to spring
out and maim and kill. It is completely beyond our
control.

T HIS PICTURE OF ANGER DESCRIBES WELL those
moments in our lives when we suddenly feel as though
we've lost control. We're like wild animal tamers standing
inside the cage, chairs raised, whips cracking, as we fight
off this uncontrollable beast. But occasionally when we're

tired or when our attention is diverted for a moment, the tiger springs out. Then we must recapture the animal with great effort, and return it to the cage where we carefully guard its every movement.

If you feel this way about controlling your anger, *beware*. Thinking of anger in these terms permits us to do many things that are wrong. It excuses inexcusable behavior. It justifies the unjustifiable.

Anger Under Control

While we may be satisfied with thinking of our anger as uncontrollable, this view is inconsistent with what the Bible says. The Bible never portrays anger as a wild beast beyond our control. In fact, Proverbs exalts the man who controls his anger: "It is better to be slow-tempered than famous; it is better to have self-control than to control an army" (16:32). And the preacher in Ecclesiastes warns, "Don't be quick-tempered—that is being a fool" (7:9). The Bible says that we have a choice—we can either be quick to anger or slow to anger. We make the choice. And thus it is in our power to change the way we react to situations.

But we don't like this idea. It makes us responsible for much that we would rather not be responsible for. It calls us to account for activities we would like to get away with. It makes us feel guilty and puts the heavy hand on us to change our actions—if we really want to.

But sometimes we don't want to hold back our anger—we feel we need to stay angry for certain reasons. Let's look at four of them:

1. First, *we get results when we get angry*. Often when

we control our anger and seek to deal with issues in a calm, quiet manner, we don't seem to get the results we want.

A few years ago my oldest boy, David, came home from school with a severely strained back. He had been practicing front flips in gym class and the teacher, concerned that he might land wrong, jerked on the safety harness, suspending him in midair with his back down. Since he had used a springboard to jump, he was high in the air and the jolt really hurt his back. The doctor prescribed therapy that lasted eight days and cost a bundle.

When I spoke to the representatives for the school about their responsibility to share the cost, they made it plain they would do nothing. Even though I was upset with them, I felt no need to rant and rave at their action. I informed them that I would find out exactly what had happened, and that we would probably sue them. They sent an insurance adjuster to speak with me. I again told them I would take the issue to court unless they covered my medical expenses. They stalled. Because I stated my intentions calmly, they did not believe that I would, in fact, act. Even after I warned them not to take my easygoing disposition as lack of willingness to fight, they continued to stall.

Finally, we were able to work things out. Yet, after the whole thing was resolved, I couldn't help feeling that I would have gotten it settled faster had I come in furious, yelling about their unfair treatment. It often seems easier to get results when we show great anger.

2. Second, *our anger gives us power over others*. In some ways this is similar to our first reason. No one likes

to deal with an angry person. Most people give in a little to satisfy an angry person because they're afraid what he might do if they don't appease him. As a result, an angry person gains power over others. He uses his anger to get what he wants—even when he isn't truly angry about a particular situation.

When Bob and Dorothy came in for counseling they were ready to split up. In fact, she was already chasing him out of the house occasionally. The problem was his anger. When he didn't like something, no matter how small the issue, he exploded in anger. The kids left the house as soon as he came home because they didn't want to deal with him. But when I showed him what his anger was doing at home and suggested change, he was frightened. "How can I get anything done without anger? No one will respect me if I don't get angry to show them I mean business. My father ruled our house with anger. I just don't see how a man can be a man at home without getting angry." He clearly knew that anger means power in our relationships.

3. Third, *we may enjoy feeling resentful after someone hurts us.* That may sound strange, but sometimes it's true. We may enjoy going away from the scene of our anger and mentally reviewing our injury. Each time we review what happened we get angry all over again. We can think of the incident any time or place, because no one knows what's going on inside our minds.

We may particularly enjoy the feeling of superiority that comes from resenting what someone did to us. We can tell ourselves that we never would have acted like that. We're too good to behave so abominably. So we not only enjoy our resentment, but we also enjoy the feeling of superiority our resentment brings.

4. Finally, *we get angry because we don't know any other effective problem-solving methods.* As Gale and Rene shared with me in premarital counseling, both admitted that anger played a key role in the break-up of their first marriages. I shared with them a problem-solving method that minimizes the effect of anger. "Boy, why didn't somebody share this with us before?" they asked when I finished. No one ever told them you can solve problems without getting angry. Because most people never develop good problem-solving skills, they turn to anger as the simplest alternative. While the results might often be negative, it's still the only method they know.

Anger is a choice you make based on your judgment of a situation. The chemical-physiological response in our bodies that we associate with anger is actually associated with a variety of emotions. You can generate the same response by being involved in a challenging game of tennis, or by getting thoroughly involved in a dramatic television program. We respond with anger not because of what happens inside our bodies, but because in our minds *we think* we should get angry in a certain situation.

Psychology and the Bible on Anger
Certain psychological approaches to anger are significantly different from biblical views. The Bible, written for the common person, speaks of the average person's conception of anger—the *obvious* feelings and actions of rage.

On the other hand, many psychologists search for the

starting place for anger, tracing our feelings back to their initial stages. At these stages, most people are unaware of feeling angry, and simply feel slightly uncomfortable. The assumption of psychologists is that the earlier we sense anger the more quickly we can deal with it. And the quicker we deal with it, the fewer problems it will cause for us.

There are apparent contradictions between these two approaches that form a wide gap. Today many psychologists see anger as a natural emotion that we should simply accept as part of life. On the other hand the Bible condemns most anger, leaving space for only carefully controlled anger at oppression and unrighteousness. We must admit that the initial stirrings that may lead to anger are natural, and that there's nothing we can do to prevent them. In this we agree with those psychologists. However, beyond this point we *can* control our anger and actions. When we sense these initial stirrings, we can make decisions whether or not we will get angry later on.

The brain is the mechanism that helps us decide whether anger is justified or not. Pre-anger arousal is a natural response to frustration, rejection, fear, and humiliation. But nothing demands that we actually get angry. Our arousal just gives us the physical capacity to deal with the situation in the event that it becomes dangerous and requires us to get involved and solve the problem immediately.

Actually, we decide to get angry or remain calm based on what we tell ourselves about the situation (our self-talk).

When we encounter a situation that displeases us, we

tell ourselves, "I want this situation to be a certain way." But we also say, "I'm not getting what I want." When this happens we react by telling ourselves, "It's horrible not to get what I want." This reaction by itself would not be too harmful even though it's far from correct. However, when we tell ourselves, "I must have my way," we often follow this with, "Since someone else is preventing me from getting my own way, I'm going to punish that person." Our anger then becomes their punishment. We lash out to make certain we'll get our way.

Seen in this light, anger is a choice to use an emotional reaction rather than effective problem-solving techniques. It is a rejection of rational techniques in favor of rage. We use it like a steamroller to squash others' arguments to make sure we "win."

After we've been angry, we often increase our anger or sustain it by talking to ourselves about what happened. We review how badly Sue mistreated us, or the terrible things Frank said about us. If we were no different from animals (who do not have our capacity for memory), we would quickly get over our anger. But instead our minds go over and over the time of anger, creating all sorts of emotional frustrations and problems.

Part of Christian maturity, however, is putting away anger. This theme is prominent in the Bible. God does not want us to stay angry. Why not? In Galatians 5:20 Paul tells us that anger is one of the fruits of the flesh. It results from allowing Satan's influence to predominate over the Holy Spirit's. James tells us that anger cannot accomplish God's purposes for our lives. "Anger doesn't make us good, as God demands we must be" (1:20).

If you want the Holy Spirit to work in and through your life, you must put away anger as a way of handling problems and conflict. And it's not easy. You need to replace your anger-generating thoughts with peace-, patience-, and joy-generating thoughts. You need to replace your angry reactions with more effective problem-solving tools.

Overcoming Anger

We overcome anger by viewing life from God's perspective. While God gets angry, he never gets angry for the wrong reasons or loses control. When he gets angry it is always a righteous anger. Thus if we can learn how to view life from his perspective, we will defuse the thoughts that lead us to the kind of sinful anger that blows our relationships apart.

There are three things to remember:

1. *God is sufficient for all our needs*. If he is sufficient for our needs, then we are wrong to get angry because our needs are not met. He gives us all that is coming to us in this life—and less. He withholds the punishment we deserve and showers us with blessings. So when we begin to talk with ourselves about being deprived, we need to remind ourselves that God gives us all we need.

A few years ago, at a pastor's conference, I met Fred, a minister in a small-town church. After many hours of discussion together, he really opened up to me and shared how he often struggled with his needs and their conflict with his wants. He often felt deprived because his small church couldn't pay a large enough salary to meet the wants of his life. I urged him to go back and look up

Romans 8:32 when this happens. And years later he wrote, "It works! Slowly my upset feelings about my wants recede into the background, and I begin to thank God for what he's already given me."

2. *God rules over the events of our lives.* Any time we talk about suffering and affliction, we come back to Romans 8:28. No matter what we face, God is with us. And he's not a passive observer, watching events that interest him but do not involve him. He is there as an active participant, controlling and working on our behalf to take the worst that life has to offer and create something of value out of it.

When I begin to talk to myself about how unfairly I've been treated, I switch about-face and focus my attention on the Holy Spirit who is working on my behalf. I remind myself that no matter what happens, the Holy Spirit is great enough to create something of value out of it. That being true, I find I have no reason to get angry.

About six years ago I was fired from a staff position in a large suburban church, a position I'd prepared for throughout most of my adult life. The dismissal struck me as a disaster of unbelievable proportions, but the Holy Spirit slowly changed my perspective. I learned to focus on who God is, what he could do. Even in the midst of my pain, I could see the Holy Spirit working, affirming me as a person. Even in six years I can see many things he did through that firing that could not have been accomplished without it.

3. *Nothing is more important than my relationship with Jesus Christ.* No matter how battered and bruised I might be on the outside, no external event can separate me from

the love of God in Jesus Christ. Paul concludes the eighth chapter of Romans by asking, "Who can separate us from God's love in Christ?" And what is the answer? "No one. Nothing." As I'm knocked around by the storms of life, I know my relationship with Jesus Christ remains constant from his end. I just have to focus on maintaining my end. And this relationship is what matters, for it is the only thing I will take with me from this life.

God's perspective also involves expecting to be treated as Jesus was. I frequently operate under the assumption that if I do right, then people will treat me right. But look at Jesus! How did people treat him? "We despised him and rejected him—a man of sorrows, acquainted with bitterest grief. We turned our backs on him and looked the other way when he went by. He was despised and we didn't care" (Isaiah 53:3). Yet this is the only man who ever lived without sin!

In John 15:20 Jesus warns his disciples, "A slave isn't greater than his master! So since they persecuted me, naturally they will persecute you." This means that each rejection or humiliation we receive as a result of living as a Christian identifies us as Jesus' disciples. When we feel angry at our mistreatment, God's perspective says, "Rejoice. These events declare your status as a child of God, just as they did in Jesus' life."

If we look through God's eyes, we see that Christian growth comes through suffering. The way we think is all too human—if we live for God and do what he wants, life will be a super highway. But God tells us that all of life is a back country road, full of ruts and potholes. We learn to love and serve him by following his guidance through the trouble spots. James actually says, "Dear brothers, is your life full of difficulties and temptations? Then be happy, for when the way is rough, your patience has a chance to grow" (James 1:2-3).

We should never be surprised by suffering. God warns us that it will come, but, as humans, we still feel frustrated and angry when things are out of our hands. Yet, God uses these frustrations to draw us to himself and to teach us how to rejoice in the face of suffering—one of God's primary methods for growing strong Christians. When we encounter difficulties, we should talk to ourselves about how God is strengthening our Christian life rather than getting angry.

Having God's perspective also includes recognizing our responsibility to minister to our world in Jesus' name. We are not children of this world, but only aliens passing through. This means that the world will never understand us. Our values are different. Our lifestyles are different. We cannot expect a world that lives by different values to understand us.

On the other hand we have been sent by God to minister in Jesus' name. We are not simply strangers, but strangers sent to minister that people might know of the other world we desire. Instead of complaining about what we don't have, we are to give from what we do have so others might share our life in Christ. We are not here to be blessed, but to bless, not to be served, but to serve, not to receive, but to give. When angry thoughts arise because someone is mistreating us, we need to seek a way of ministering to him in Jesus' name. And as we focus on our ministry to others, causes for anger diminish. They are no longer sources of offense, but indicators of a need that we can meet.

We implement God's perspective in our lives through Spirit-guided self-talk. No matter what situation arises we can seek to view it through God's eyes. He is sufficient for our every need. We don't need to get angry any more than he did. If we have this attitude as we suffer, we become more like Jesus and less like our old sinful selves.

When this happens our anger is replaced with patience and joy. No matter what this world throws at us, we rest secure in our relationship with God. We can rejoice in the face of difficulties because we know the Holy Spirit will create good out of the worst of them. But best of all, we can offer forgiveness instead of anger.

When you operate from God's perspective, you can forgive any offense against you. Look at how Jesus responded while hanging on the cross. He cried, "Father, forgive these people, for they don't know what they are doing" (Luke 23:34a). He had God's perspective on the most tragic event in history. He knew God was big enough to create something good out of it. He knew it did not change his relationship with God. He knew that even as the perfect one, he would grow through the suffering he experienced. He knew he had been sent to minister—not to be ministered to. With that perspective, he forgave the most heinous crime in history. And with that perspective we can forgive any offense people may commit against us.

Dealing with Anger
It's nice to imagine that we will always see life from

God's perspective, but that is rather idealistic thinking. Not one of us is perfect. We all get angry sometimes. We don't always implement God's perspective. How can we handle anger under these circumstances?

1. First, most important, and most difficult—*admit it to yourself*. When you get angry, admit it first to yourself and then confess it to God and those you are angry with.

We often don't admit our anger. In fact we try to hide it because we know it's wrong. We try to hide it not only from others but also from ourselves. It is a blow to our pride when we're not in control of ourselves.

How can we expose our anger?

First, *ask the Holy Spirit for wisdom to see your anger when it is hidden from you*. David prayed, "Search me, O God, and know my heart; test my thoughts. Point out anything you find in me that makes you sad, and lead me along the path of everlasting life" (Psalm 139:23-24). James tells us that in our struggles with temptation, God welcomes our requests for wisdom (James 1:5). "If you want to know what God wants you to do, ask him, and he will gladly tell you, for he is always ready to give a bountiful supply of wisdom to all who ask him; he will not resent it." Not only will he give it, but unlike some other people, he won't make us feel bad for asking. So begin by asking the Holy Spirit's help in seeing when you're angry.

Second, *notice others' reactions to you*. Being in tune with others in your environment is vitally important, because often those around you will sense your anger, even if you don't. If people suddenly clam up when you're talking, begin to avoid you, or seem uncomfortable or fearful around you, there is a good chance that your angry emotions are showing.

Third, *take a good, long look at yourself*. You alone know what you do when you get angry. How do you respond? What devices do you use to hide your anger? Look for them. Then when you know you're angry, admit it. You may find it valuable to simply say to yourself, "I'm angry." This helps you define the churning, tension-laden feeling inside. This helps me a great deal. Once I know what I'm dealing with, I can solve the problem more easily.

2. *After you admit your anger to yourself, admit it to others*. By admitting it I'm not suggesting you attack them for causing your anger. Remember, you alone are responsible for your anger because of your self-talk. But you need to admit your anger to others so that you may both deal with it—especially if the situation of anger closely involves that person.

They probably already know you are angry. Most of us have emotional sensors highly attuned to others' anger. This is particularly true in families, where survival often depends on our ability to read another person's moods. Angry people, we assume, are dangerous, so we quickly learn to recognize anger signals. By the time you admit your anger, everyone else is probably aware of it, but too polite to say anything.

In admitting your anger, however, remember that anger is threatening. Few people want to face open anger in another. Thus it's important when you admit your anger that you also take responsibility for it. I use this formula,

"I feel angry because . . ." In this way I'm telling others, "I'm angry." I'm saying, "This anger is my responsibility." But I'm also telling them, "I'm angry because certain events impinged on my life." In doing this I'm letting them help me deal with my anger, and I'm also not putting them in the uncomfortable position of feeling at fault.

3. *Invite others to help you deal with your anger.* To make certain that others understand what I'm trying to do when I admit my anger, I say, "I feel angry because . . . Would you help me deal with it?" In doing this I'm telling them I want a solution that respects their needs. However, this does not free me from the obligation to share my needs in a calm, rational manner so we can work out a mutually agreeable solution.

By admitting anger and asking for help we challenge the idea that anger is a force inside us that we can't control. We've also discovered that anger is a choice we make in response to events around us. We can control anger by learning to view life from God's perspective. And when that fails, we can deal with our anger by admitting it and seeking a mutually acceptable solution with others. Through all of these steps we follow the biblical injunction to put away anger.

Things to Do/Think About:
1. In this chapter, we discovered some reasons why we get angry and stay that way—we like the results we get; it gives us power over others; we enjoy feeling resentful; we don't know any other effective problem-solving methods. Which one applies most frequently in your life?
2. Think about the past week. When were you angry? Write out the self-talk that led to your anger. Then write out how you could have implemented God's perspective and the three steps in dealing with anger.
3. When you realize you're angry this week, quietly admit it to a friend and ask for help in dealing with it.

5

Jonah: The Blue Prophet

"I DON'T KNOW HOW YOU CAN CALL yourself a Christian, Jean Ann," scolded Aleta, the wife of a regional executive minister. "Christians have absolutely no cause for depression. They should be filled with the joy of the Lord."

Over the past seven years, Jean Ann, a minister's wife from a small town in northern Wisconsin, has been hospitalized six times for attempted suicide and severe depression. During that time she's been under a psychiatrist's care and has received weekly counseling for her problems. Her husband refuses to admit there's a problem and says, "It's all in her head. If she'd just straighten up, everything would be all right." She can't seem to "straighten up" so quickly and easily, but she is slowly making progress.

Can a Christian be depressed, particularly for a long time? "Maybe," we say grudgingly. But if there's one thing we Christians seem to be certain about, it's that our Bible heroes were never depressed. We see depression as a relatively modern problem.

Let's take a look at the life of a prophet whose story makes up a colorful book of the Bible—Jonah. Most of the time when we look at his life we watch with astonishment as God works one of the great miracles of the Old Testament. Jonah's life is a great Old Testament missionary story. But there is another perspective. Jonah was a man with emotions just like ours. Based on the symptoms he displayed, I believe he was a man who was subject to severe depression.

Jonah's Symptoms of Depression

Jonah showed a number of the common symptoms of depression. He slept in the ship's hold while the sailors did everything in their power to save the boat and themselves from drowning. Depressed people commonly sleep excessively. Although they may also struggle with insomnia, they can often sleep right through a major crisis. Why? Because sleep is the original tranquilizer. It temporarily deadens the pain of life, giving us needed relief from our suffering.

Second, Jonah attempted suicide. Let's look at him in a different light for a moment. When the sailors cast lots to see who was responsible for the storm and their plight, God directed the lot to Jonah. At this point Jonah admitted he was responsible for their troubles. The solution was simple. All Jonah had to do was submit to God's will and say he would go to Ninevah just as soon as the boat reached dry land.

But he didn't! Instead he told the sailors, "Save the boat by throwing me overboard." He so strongly resisted God's will that he chose to die rather than to do what God wanted. However, God thwarted Jonah's suicide by having him swallowed by the fish. While in the belly of the great fish, Jonah at last realized he could not avoid God's will—he had to do it. And he did do it as soon as he hit dry land. Although he obeyed, he didn't change into a happy, willing person all at once. Later he responded with pouting and anger because God forced him to preach to the Ninevites, a group of people he didn't like. And finally, he actually challenged God to kill him if he disapproved of Jonah's behavior—another possible suicide attempt.

Third, Jonah's view of the world was bleak. He also engaged in foolish self-pity. Imagine him sitting on the hillside outside Ninevah waiting for God's wrath to shower down on the city. As he sat there the sun beat down on him uncomfortably. God allowed a plant to grow up and give him shade, but then permitted a worm to kill the plant so Jonah would again suffer from the heat. Jonah complained loudly of his discomfort, and when God challenged him about his anger, he retorted, "I do well to be angry." And why was he angry? Because the plant—that God had mercifully given him in the first place to shade him—had died. Foolish self-pity combined with a bleak view of the world created Jonah's depression.

Let's give Jonah a little credit. He did suppress his anger at God—for a while. But we cannot properly understand the Book of Jonah without seriously considering the last chapter, the chapter that tells the rest of the story. Jonah fled from God not because he thought preaching in Ninevah would be a difficult chore, but because he hated the Ninevites and did not want them to repent and experience God's mercy. When God forced him to preach to them and then graciously responded to their repentance, Jonah was bitterly angry. Long-term anger, especially when it contains elements of hatred or deep bitterness toward others, leads to depression. Jonah's anger flared out in the final chapter—a deep-seated, bitter anger, directed against God because he hated the Ninevites while God treated them with mercy.

Spiritual Reasons for Jonah's Depression

Depression often has a spiritual base. Let's look at Jonah for an example. Why was he depressed?

1. He was depressed because *he fought God's known will for his life*. When we actively resist God's will for our lives, we often experience depression. Our resistance also produces guilt, and the only way to deal with guilt is through repentance. As long as we refuse to repent, we continue to be depressed. (This is only true for those who care what God thinks about their lives.)

2. Jonah was depressed because *he resented God's plan for his life*. If we resent a major component of our lives, we get depressed. If you don't like the way you look, if you aren't pleased with your abilities, if you don't like the home you grew up in, if you feel God is forcing you to

do things you don't want to do, you'll feel depressed. Why? Because when we think God is being unfair with us, depression is the result. Through self-talk we are saying to ourselves, "This is not fair. God has cheated me. God is mistreating me." But when a person actively resists his Creator and Redeemer, he gets depressed. Peace and joy come only as we submit to God's plan for our lives—knowing that no matter how difficult it might be, it's still best because our heavenly Father never gives us anything other than what's best.

3. He was depressed because *he resented God's concern for Nineveh*. To understand this we need to enter into the prophet's age. Nineveh was the capital of Assyria. For years the Assyrians oppressed the Israelites. There was nothing the Israelites wanted more than to see God annihilate them. Jonah, an Israelite, hated the Assyrians as much as many Americans hate the Russians, but he was called by God to preach to them. Jonah, however, had seen God work in the past. He knew that God is slow to anger and quick to show mercy. He knew that if the Ninevites repented, God would turn aside his judgment—just as he did. Jonah didn't want that to happen. He thought that would be unfair to Israel, which had suffered too much at Assyria's hands. He didn't want to turn the situation over to God, the righteous judge.

Even though we may be powerless to correct it, injustice often stirs up our anger. And, if we also feel personally mistreated and helpless, we tend to stuff the anger down inside and let it churn. There's no better way to cause our own depression.

4. Jonah was depressed because *he engaged in self-pity*

through negative self-talk. Jonah was very good at self-pity, but not very good at forgiveness. As a result he talked himself more deeply into depression. Often, before the onset of depression, a person engages in negative, self-pitying, self-talk. "I'm no good. Life's not fair. I wish there were something about me I could like. I wish I didn't have to do this. I wish I were somewhere else. I'm a failure." We may go on and on, putting ourselves down in our self-talk. The result is depression. The more self-pitying self-talk you engage in, the more depressed you'll become. And the more depressed you become, the more you'll pity yourself. It's a vicious cycle.

Challenging Depression

God cured Jonah's depression just as he can cure ours. How? First, he challenged Jonah's view of reality. Let's go back to Jonah's bleak view of the world for a moment. He was outside the city of Nineveh sulking because God had shown mercy on the Ninevites. He made a leafy shelter to shade himself, but it began to wither in the heat. God helped him out by sprouting a vine with broad leaves that grew quickly to shade him. But the next morning God sent a worm that ate the stem of the plant and killed it. Then God sent a scorching east wind. Jonah felt more and more faint as the sun climbed in the sky. Then he got angry and said, "Death is better than this!"

God knew Jonah was overreacting. He asked, "Is it right for you to be angry because the plant died?"

And even though Jonah retorted with a childishly smart-aleck remark, "Yes, it is; it is right for me to be angry enough to die!" we can tell that God made his point.

Jonah realized the foolishness of being more concerned about a shade plant than about the lives of the Ninevites (4:10-11).

As God challenged Jonah's view of reality, so *we can challenge our view of reality by using God's Word.* When we're depressed, we view the world through dark glasses. We see the bad in almost everything. In fact, we become so negative, it's difficult to see the good. But in Philippians 4:8 Paul tells us, "Fix your thoughts on what is true and good and right. Think about things that are pure and lovely, and dwell on the fine, good things in others. Think about all you can praise God for and be glad about."

God's Word challenges our view of reality. There's much in life we can do little about, events we cannot control. But we can control our thinking about those events. We can look on the bright side—or the negative side. The one leads to peace and joy, the other to depression.

When I was fired from that job I really enjoyed a few years ago, I heard myself saying, "You're a failure. You're no good as a minister."

Then I realized what I was saying. Each time I heard those negative thoughts, I challenged them. "No, you're not! You may be a failure at this church, but you're not a failure in many other areas." Slowly but surely I overcame my depression by focusing on the good and pure and right.

When we begin to focus on the parts of our life that disturb us, we need to remind ourselves that God has placed them there (or has allowed them to come into our lives) *for a purpose.* We need to accept the unchangeable as his will for us at the present because he wants to teach us lessons or minister through us in a way that demands these things be present. On the other hand, we need to bear with the changeable while we work at changing them, again recognizing that God permits these things for a reason.

After I was fired I moved, through the Holy Spirit's leading, into my present position in a church in northern Michigan. It's a small church that sometimes can barely meet my family's needs. I've struggled here for five years, much of the time looking for another position but never feeling that God's timing was right for me to make a move. I know I am here for a reason and this is where God wants me to be. At times it's very difficult, but each time I begin getting down, I talk to myself about God's power and his will as my Lord. He knows best. And in the long run, that's what matters most.

When we indulge in self-pity, we challenge God's loving concern for us. When we begin to bad-talk our lives and surroundings, we're really saying to God, "You don't quite know what you're doing. Take a little advice from me and straighten this problem out and everything will be all right." We need to remind ourselves constantly about God's love and concern, because if we resist his will, depression is sure to follow.

Finally, *we need to realize that much of the suffering and hardship of life is a result of God's discipline.* "For when he punishes you, it proves that he loves you. When he whips you it proves you are really his child" (Hebrews 12:6). Instead of fighting the difficulties and struggling against them, we can recognize each one as a friend, sent by God to bring us to maturity in Christ (James 1:2-4).

Suffering is one of God's primary tools for developing Christian character. As we realize this truth and talk to ourselves about it when we get discouraged, we can slowly overcome the depression that comes from resisting God.

Looking at Jonah's life we only see one small aspect of depression. Depression has social and biological causes as well as spiritual/psychological causes. Chemical changes in our bodies through either natural means or through drug use can produce depression. So can great social changes. Depression is often our natural response to a major loss. We don't want to leave these causes unacknowledged—many times depressed people need professional counselors, doctors, psychiatrists, or psychologists. But in this book we will deal mostly with the spiritual/psychological aspects of depression.

Things to Do/Think About:
1. Read the Book of Jonah in the light of what you learned in this chapter.
2. Sometime this week when you're feeling "down," write out your self-talk. How does it contribute to your depression? Figure out what self-talk can lift your spirits. Then write down one or two positive self-talk phrases and tape them on a mirror, the refrigerator door, or the dashboard of your car.

For Further Reading:
John White, *The Masks of Melancholy* (InterVarsity)

6
Dealing with Depression

RANK THESE THREE MAJOR EMOTIONS—worry, anger, and depression. Which one causes the most problems?

Depression. Surprised? Because you see anger and worry more frequently than depression, you may think they cause more problems. But mental health experts agree that depression creates more problems than either anger or worry.

This fact may not be obvious to us because depression is so internal, hiding inside our minds. When we feel depressed, we speak largely of the symptoms, rarely recognizing the depression itself. In addition, we view depression as a "sick" emotion, an emotion "good people" don't have.

Because depression afflicts so many, we need to learn how to deal with it. When left unchecked, it saps our strength, strips the joy from our lives, and keeps us from being productive. And, until we deal directly with our depression rather than just focusing on its symptoms, we won't regain our lost strength and joy.

Types of Depression

In order to understand the situation better, let's define three basic types of depression. First, *chronic depression* is basically depression as a permanent way of life. It is a long-term problem, frequently learned through the family situation or culture we grow up in. Each family creates its own distinctive culture or outlook on life. Some focus solely on the bad, complain about how others use and abuse them, and concentrate on the negative while overlooking the good. This kind of family develops serious, unresolved conflict, and its members grow up learning how to be depressed as a general approach to life.

Eric and Ruth made an impression on me from the day I met them. But unfortunately it was the wrong kind. They never said anything good about anyone and always had a story to share about someone mistreating them. Both their children went through difficult divorces. The whole family keyed in on life's faults, ignoring its blessings. I believe they suffered from chronic depression.

A second type of depression is *situational depression*. This has a shorter duration than chronic depression and may come and go depending on circumstances. People with situational depression tend to look back on times when they did not feel depressed, saying, "When I get out of this into a more normal situation, I will no longer feel depressed." Family, work, church, and neighborhood situations can all create a climate for this type of depression.

One pastor related this story to me: "For the past three years I have tried to move from my present job. However, pastoral relocation in my denomination grows increasingly difficult each year. My church, with its congregation of mostly retired people, does not seem interested in growth. I feel my pastoral skills, especially in evangelism and church growth, no longer relate to my job situation. But I know my depression will leave when I relocate. At the present I do my best, yet I still struggle."

I regularly feel depressed in April and May. We live in northern Michigan with its long winters. By the time April and May drag in, I strain at the bit to get outside and enjoy outdoor life, but rain and cold keep me inside. I don't get enough sunlight to combat depression, nor do I get the fresh fruits and vegetables my body needs. Sometimes I feel trapped by my home and its limited resources. All these events and factors create a situation where I feel depressed. A month later, the situation changes, and I feel fine.

This other pastor and I both suffer from situational depression. I believe most people—at some time in their lives—do also.

A third type of depression is *crisis depression*. Crisis depression temporarily follows a major loss in our lives—death of a loved one, loss of a job, an accident, a fire, or anything we might call a major loss. Crisis depression is God's shock absorber, helping us cope with life as our inner resources recover their strength. A natural response, crisis depression should cause no shame.

Sources of Depression
We've probably all experienced one of these kinds of depression, but we may not know just how it came about. Depression has different causes, some of which may be biological factors only a doctor can discover and treat. But more frequently, depression grows out of negative self-talk and self-pity when we confront a situation that creates a climate for depression.

Depression usually has a basis in reality, but we can severely complicate or worsen our depression by our self-talk. We lead ourselves into depression if we continually tell ourselves how difficult our lives are, how others mistreat us and take advantage of us, and how we need assistance others won't give, and how we face more than we can stand. Our constant theme becomes: Life should be better than it is. The more we repeat this story to ourselves, the worse our depression gets and the more bad we see as a result.

Nora is a good example. Her husband died. She had to move from her nice home in the country to a small apartment in town. She missed her husband's companionship. Her friends didn't visit as much now that he was gone. Her children didn't visit often enough. She was sure that if she didn't quit smoking, cancer would kill her. The refrain never changed, and her depression deepened. Within a few years she died a premature death. I believe that her depression was a contributing factor.

While this general pattern often accounts for depression, other specific factors may bring about the same result. *Unresolved guilt often leads to depression.* When I do something wrong, I tell myself how bad I am, how others would think less of me if they knew. I say, "I'm a horrible person. If other people discovered my sin, they would consider me a low-life—they would reject me. How can God love someone like me?" I love to talk myself down.

That's tragic. God gave us a conscience to draw us back to him. He does not want us to just feel guilty when we sin, but to repent. The moment we sin, he wants us to confess and ask his forgiveness. He wants us to pray to be refilled with his Spirit and to resolve by his Spirit to stop our sin. When we don't repent, unresolved guilt creates depression.

Even more tragic, some guilt is false. If we establish a false standard of righteousness we can't meet, we will surely feel guilty when we "fail." Many homemakers establish unrealistic standards for their homes' upkeep, then feel guilty about having a messy house when someone comes over. Most parents set up standards no one could meet, but feel guilty when they, or their children, "fall short." Many men and women create impossible standards for work, then berate themselves for not accomplishing more. If guilt plagues us and we regularly fail to meet our standards, we need to evaluate our standards (a friend's counsel may help).

In addition, *unresolved anger, bitterness, or resentment often creates depression.* I dreaded visiting Penny. Each time I entered her mobile home she recited her litany of woes. Her children mistreated her. No one visited her. Her husband died too young. Her health gave her problems. She was losing weight, and the doctor couldn't stop it. If he knew his job, he could help her. Her blood pressure was too high. Her doctors were incompetent. Her trailer needed repairs, but repairmen were either inept or thieves.

Underneath the complaints was an angry, bitter woman who felt that God had cheated her by taking away her husband, that her children had neglected her by living their own lives. Because she felt it was not right to get angry with God, she couldn't even talk to God about her anger. Because she feared her children would visit even less, she was all sugar and spice when they visited, hiding her true feelings. As a result, deep depression started growing.

We often upbraid ourselves for our feelings, but do nothing about them. Instead we keep going over and over the same thoughts in our minds: "I don't think he should treat me like that." "I shouldn't be feeling this way." "No one ever takes my views into consideration." "He cheated me." "He hurt me." And many more. An angry person who has never come to terms with his anger, who has let anger grow into sustained resentment and bitterness, usually feels depressed.

Unresolved fears also lead to depression. One of my church members told me about her next-door neighbor, LouAnn. Every time a storm warning flashed across the screen of her television set, it terrified her. She would pace around the house, looking out the windows, waiting in fear for the storm that might be coming.

Even though the warning originated 100 miles away, and the last damaging storm in her area attacked thirty years ago, LouAnn still got frightened whenever the wind blew hard. As she waited, her spirits would sink. She would tell herself about all the bad things storms can bring. Her unresolved fears helped her get depressed.

All of us worry about what might happen to our children, how we might lose our job, how rain might ruin the big ball game, how the car might break down while we are traveling through the inner city, how people might dislike us if we speak our mind. Fear controls many people's lives, and unresolved fear creates depression.

Symptoms of Depression

Many people don't recognize depression. Just as there are many possible causes of depression, there are also a number of obvious results or symptoms. It is important to recognize these side effects so we can take future steps to overcome depression and put it out of our lives. Here are a few of the symptoms:

1. *Sadness.* Depression makes it difficult to be happy or see humor in anything.

2. *Fatigue.* Depression makes us feel tired even when we do little, and even after we've rested.

3. *Unusual sleeping habits.* Some people sleep too much. They can lie down anytime, anywhere and sleep, even after a good night's sleep. Others can't fall asleep even when desperately tired.

4. *Eating problems.* Some people eat to overcome depression. For others, even their favorite food loses its taste.

5. *A negative self-image*. A depressed person down-grades himself. He sees all his faults through a magnifying glass, but views his strengths through the wrong end of a telescope.

6. *Difficulty concentrating*. A depressed person's mind refuses to focus on any subject for more than a short time.

7. *A driving or compulsive lifestyle*. Many people hide depression behind too much activity. I work extensively with the recently divorced, an often depressed population. As they run from their depression, they often maintain a social life that would kill the average person.

8. *Multiple physical complaints*. Nothing major, just always something wrong. If a doctor finds anything wrong and cures it, a short time later something else goes wrong. We just don't feel up to par.

Many of these symptoms give either temporary escape or relief from depression. Eating and sleeping don't cure depression, but they feel good. And for the depressed, any relief—no matter how temporary—is welcome.

What Depression Does to Us
Depression creates a world of muted tones—black, gray, brown. It literally changes our view of life.

I'm quite light sensitive and have to wear sunglasses whenever I drive or I get headaches. Sometimes when I drive I think a storm is developing, but when I lift my glasses, I find they have created a deceptive picture. I think of depression as putting sunglasses on our view of life.

Depression also affects those around us. First, we withdraw from contact with others. In the days immediately following my dismissal from my church pastorate, I simply hid from people. In my depression I did not want to see others. But I discovered this withdrawal hurts others who love us and want to help. It can alienate them, making them angry with us.

However, some depressed people move in the opposite direction. They depend too much on others. They can't make a decision without seeking support from someone else. They need encouragement to do the simplest act. Because others want to live their own lives, this dependency is often irritating and upsetting.

The depressed frequently depress those near them. It's almost as if depression were a communicable disease. Others sense this and flee, compounding the problem.

We may even complicate our depression by blaming others for our problems. When many things go wrong all at once, we often look for someone to blame so we can duck the responsibility ourselves. Others react with astonishment and outrage because they have not changed, but suddenly we blame them for our troubles. Remember Penny? The more she blamed others for her problems, the less people visited her. Yet she needed those people to push away her depression.

We also hurt ourselves when we feel depressed. The most frequent harm comes from negative self-talk, when we badmouth ourselves. Or we may try to solve our negative feelings about ourselves by fleeing into the dead-end street of perfectionism. We hope to hide our defects in order to win the favor of others, however, we end up setting unrealistic standards for ourselves that lead to unresolved guilt and further depression. Some people may even resort to drugs, such as marijuana, crack, heroin, alcohol, or tranquilizers to keep them from feeling the reality of their depression.

As a last resort, many depressed people think about suicide, and some actually try it. The prophet Jonah not only thought about it but tried to end his life. Only God's action stopped him. Suicidal thoughts grow out of our feelings of low self-esteem.

You should not be ashamed for having thought about suicide. But when you do it is important to talk to a minister or professional counselor. Most important, you should realize that whether depression is severe or just beginning, there are steps you can take to overcome your depression.

Overcoming Depression

How do we overcome depression? Some depression requires medical attention. But trust in a loving, sovereign, all-powerful God will overcome most depression. God sent Jesus to die for our sins, a tremendous demonstration of love. If God loved us that much when we opposed him, how much more must he love us when we become his children! Our loving heavenly Father promises to give his children everything they need for living an abundant life. But abundant does not mean pain-free.

When we recognize the symptoms of depression, we need to focus our self-talk on our loving heavenly Father. There's an old song that says, "Count your blessings." It's a good idea! Actively talk to yourself about God's love and provision for your life. When you sense yourself slipping into the swamp of self-pity, tell yourself how

God meets needs in your life. When you sense anger at mistreatment, talk to yourself about how God treats you far better than you deserve. When you sense yourself slipping into fear, talk to yourself about how God promises to meet your every need, including those that are the objects of your fear. When life overwhelms you, focus on your loving heavenly Father's blessings. He gives us as much good as he thinks we can handle. Focus on the fact that God does not want you to fail, and that he will lift you up before you succumb.

Second, when you recognize the symptoms of depression, think of God's purpose in your life. He is actively working to re-create the character of his son, Jesus Christ, in you. God uses your circumstances to produce in you the fruit of love, joy, peace, long-suffering, endurance, gentleness, and the other fruits of the spirit characteristic of Jesus' life.

When I go through very painful periods in my life, I cling to God's purpose, and pray it will make me more like Jesus. Then slowly my depression lifts as I see God in charge, using an event to help me mature as a Christian.

Instead of responding in anger to life's upsets, we need to remember that God is working to create Jesus' character in us. When we face fears, we need to talk to ourselves about God's power that could protect his son in the midst of a storm. When the burdens of life seem more than we can bear, we need to remember who God is and what his purposes are for stretching us to our limits—he wants to show us how to live like Jesus.

Finally, in the face of depression, we need to tell ourselves that we never face anything God can't handle. No matter what we face, God is working in the midst of it, creating good. He called us according to his purpose, and we have responded in love. That means he is always there, no matter how roughly life might treat us.

Few people have faced as depressing a situation as Joseph, the Old Testament patriarch. His brothers sold him into slavery, his master's wife falsely accused him of attempted rape, and even his friends deserted him once they left prison. Yet at the end of his life he looked back on his trials and said, "God meant it for good."

When I face fear, anger, stress, and self-pity, I worship before God who handles all my problems. As I glory in his presence, life diminishes to a size I can handle.

Freedom from Depression

What happens when I talk positively to myself like this? I gain freedom from depression and a radical new outlook on life. My view of God changes from vindictive judge to loving heavenly Father.

In our depression we often view God as a heavenly traffic cop, waiting for us to make a mistake so he can hurl his thunderbolts at us and gleefully watch us suffer. As we gain freedom from depression, we see God as a tender father who helps us when we fall, who wants our success even more than we do, and who works to ensure it.

In addition, our view of the world changes from bleak and barren to beautiful and abundant. When we remove the dark glasses from our spiritual vision, we suddenly see the sun shining, as God pours out his blessing on our lives—even if the blessing comes in the midst of pain. Our reactions toward others change from fear of rejection to warmer, more trusting relationships. When we are depressed, we think the whole world is fighting against us. When depression lifts, we relate to people *as they are* because we become more comfortable with *who we are*.

Our view of ourselves changes. As we begin to accept the good and the bad in our lives, recognizing that God is working through both, we find that we no longer dislike ourselves.

Depression is the most complicated emotion we deal with in this book. Many depressions require professional help, particularly depressions lasting more than six months. Doctors now have anti-depressant drugs that relieve the more severe symptoms of depression. I believe taking these drugs is neither morally wrong or against Christian principles. In fact, really the opposite is true—failure to use them when you need them is throwing away help God wants to give you through modern medicine. As with other medications, anti-depressants are simply designed to deal with a biological mix-up that creates illness, in this instance *depression*.

However all depressions can be helped, in different degrees, by the principles in this chapter. Unfortunately, self-help books can only deal with everyday-type depressions, not deep-seated ones. If your struggle with depression lasts for more than six months, I urge you to seek out a trusted counselor or medical professional to help you deal with your problem.

Things to Do/Think About:
1. What are the three major sources of depression in your life? List them in your journal or on a piece of paper.
2. List the symptoms of depression that occur in your life.

3. Write three statements about who God is that will help you when you feel depressed.

For Further Reading:
Frederic Flach, *The Secret Strength of Depression* (Bantam)
H. Norman Wright, *An Answer to Depression* (Harvest House)

7

When I Feel Trapped by Guilt

BRENT BOUNCED AROUND THE HOUSE, excited. Grandma and Grandpa had invited him to spend the weekend—a birthday treat. They also invited his sister, Randi, to share in the celebration. As Brent wiggled with anticipation, he kept asking, "I wonder what they'll give me this year?"

At lunch, Grandma carried in a big birthday cake while Grandpa slipped a box, gift-wrapped, across the table. Brent picked it up, listened for a rattle, then tore off the paper. In the box was a wrist rocket—a sophisticated slingshot!

Brent delighted in his grandfather's tales of his exploits with a slingshot. He squirmed in his seat while everyone finished eating birthday cake and ice cream. He wanted to get out into Grandpa's woods to play.

After lunch, Grandpa offered to show him how to use it. "I don't need any practice. I know how to use a slingshot," claimed Brent, trotting off toward the woods. He spent the whole afternoon there, shooting at everything imaginable, hitting nothing. As he trudged slowly back to the house, discouraged, and entered the yard, Grandma's duck waddled across his path. He pulled the slingshot from his pocket, loaded a pellet, drew it back, and hit the duck square in the head. It dropped—dead.

Frightened, he pulled the duck behind the woodpile where he threw a few logs over it. He straightened from his chore only to see Randi standing inside the barn door watching him. Since she said nothing, he quietly walked back to the house, hoping she hadn't seen.

After dinner Grandma asked, "Randi, would you help me with the dishes while Brent and Grandpa take a walk in the woods?"

Randi replied, "Brent already told me he wants to do the dishes tonight, so I think I'll walk in the woods with Grandpa."

Brent's head jerked up in astonishment, but Randi whispered, "Remember the duck."

Brent did the dishes.

After breakfast next morning, Grandma said, "Randi, would you like to go shopping with me? Grandpa's going to take Brent fishing."

Randi quickly responded, "Brent told me he wants to go shopping with you so I can go fishing with Grandpa."

Brent went shopping.

That afternoon as Grandma worked around the kitchen, Brent wandered in. With hanging head he told her, "Grandma, yesterday after I came back from the woods, I shot your duck with my slingshot. I hid it behind the woodpile."

"I know, Brent. I saw you do it. I was standing at the kitchen window washing dishes. I just wondered how long you were going to let Randi make you her slave."

A Troubled Conscience

Many people live in bondage to a dead duck hidden long ago behind a woodpile. They've suffered for years because of it. They would do anything to free themselves because a troubled conscience burdens their lives.

How tragic. Christian growth is nearly impossible with a troubled conscience because it severely retards spiritual development. After King David committed adultery with the beautiful woman, Bathsheba, he wrote, "There was a time when I wouldn't admit what a sinner I was. But my dishonesty made me miserable and filled my days with frustration. All day and all night your hand was heavy on me. My strength evaporated like water on a sunny day until I finally admitted all my sins to you and stopped trying to hide them" (Psalm 32:3-5). David's troubled conscience weighed down all aspects of his life.

Proverbs 28:13 says, "A man who refuses to admit his mistakes can never be successful. But if he confesses and forsakes them, he gets another chance." A troubled conscience hinders spiritual growth and may cause a person to give up even trying to live as a Christian.

A troubled conscience also opens the door to further temptation and sin. Satan uses our memory of past sin to create a desire for more sin. He conveniently helps us overlook all the suffering our sin has caused while he reminds us of the fun we had while sinning. Or he says, "Since you've failed so often in the past, why resist now?" He uses our troubled conscience to trap us into committing more sin. Many people still see vivid pictures of sins committed during dating. Even years later, Satan will regularly rerun these old films to try to weaken them as they face current temptations.

How often during his lifetime and preaching career do you think the apostle Peter heard, "You failed Christ yourself, so how can you call on others to live in complete loyalty to him? Back off. Take it easy. Even you couldn't live a perfect life!" It must have been very difficult for Peter to keep preaching with the constant reminder of his past failure.

Troubled and Trapped

Most people don't know how to respond to a troubled conscience. Since we all sin, our lack of knowledge compounds our problem. Successful Christian living demands skill in dealing with temptation and sin.

Many people mistakenly think God deals with their sin by giving them a guilty conscience, and that their guilt with its resulting distress, atones for their sin. They think once they've suffered enough, their guilty conscience will no longer bother them. Because of their lack of understanding about forgiveness and their willingness to continue living with guilt, these people often experience some of the following negative side effects:

Fear of punishment. Brent feared Grandma's response if she learned about the dead duck. We all fear discovery when we do wrong. We fear God's anger and others' anger. As a result, we often try self-punishment to make ourselves feel better, particularly since others can't punish us when we've hidden our sin.

Depression also plays a role in a troubled conscience. We feel depressed because our sin takes something important from us, our idealized picture of who we are. We naturally respond to significant loss with depression.

Rejection. We feel rejected by God when we fail to live up to his standards. We feel rejected by others for the same reason, even when they don't know what we did. We feel rejected because we "know" how they would respond if they knew. We even reject ourselves because we don't like ourselves after we've violated our ideals.

Lowered self-esteem and feelings of worthlessness. Our self-esteem goes down when we fail. We feel worthless because we've fallen short of the standard we use to measure worth.

Feelings of isolation. When we sin, we create a terrible secret. If we share the secret with others, we feel they will reject us. Sin also isolates us from ourselves because we reject the people we actually are in favor of the people we ought to be. Feelings of isolation explain why criminals often respond to capture with, "I'm glad it's out in the open."

This complex assortment of feelings creates a troubled conscience and makes us feel miserable.

God's Way of Dealing with Sin

Many people think God punishes us for our sins with a troubled conscience. Don't believe that for a minute! God *never* punishes his children. He reserves punishment for those who reject him and his offer of salvation through Jesus Christ. Once we enter God's family, he promises never again to punish us. "There is now no condemnation [punishment] awaiting those who belong to Christ Jesus" (Romans 8:1).

But God does *discipline* us. What's the difference? Punishment is retaliation for wrongdoing. Governments punish those who violate their laws in order to protect society and the government's existence. A loving heavenly Father disciplines us because he wants to develop the character of his son, Jesus Christ. He disciplines us to bring us back to the path of righteousness where we can more fully experience his love. He disciplines as a loving father who wants to restore an erring child. God never punishes us with a troubled conscience. He troubles our conscience to call us back to himself so we will repent and ask his forgiveness.

Many people fight repentance and forgiveness. As a result sins from the past burden their present. Think of your own life. Can you recall a few past events you wish you could forget? Can you remember a few incidents where you really hurt someone? Or did something you know was wrong?

Reactions to a Troubled Conscience

People react in different ways to a troubled conscience. Some get discouraged or depressed. They punish themselves through self-pity. "Woe is me for all the wrong I've done." They behave as if self-pity, carried on long enough, makes up for their sins. Eventually their self-pity will force God to agree, "Woe is you." Then he will forgive their sins.

But God does not work that way.

Other people rebel against a troubled conscience. When they sin, their consciences bother them. How do they solve the problem? By throwing their consciences away! Because they don't want to conform, they throw out the standard that accuses them. This method does work. But they also get something they didn't bargain for—a seared conscience that no longer responds to sin.

Others deceive themselves when their conscience accuses them. "I'm not really all that bad. Look at what others do."

Bill shared with me an unusual counseling experience. A woman came for counseling who had lived 100 years of sin in her thirty years. For two hours she poured out her tale. When she finished, he told me, "I felt incredibly dirty—like someone had emptied a septic tank on me."

As he reeled under the impact of her evil life she said, "I don't understand why people look down on me. I'm not really all that bad."

We all deceive ourselves in some way about our sins.

Some people confess their sins to avoid punishment. Five-year-old Danny is a good example. He loves to play with his father's ashtray, blowing ashes all over the carpet near the coffee table. When his mother walks in, he spots her out of the corner of his eye. He runs toward her crying, "Mommy, Mommy, I'm sorry. You won't spank me, will you? I'm sorry. I'm sorry." Then he grabs her around the legs and hangs on for dear life.

Each of us, whether adult or child, has tried this technique sometime. We quickly say we are sorry to avoid punishment when we really aren't sorry for our sin. We confess to God, but next time we have the opportunity, we do the same thing. We confess only to keep God off our backs.

Many people feel remorse when they sin. They feel bad about the *consequences* of their sin, but they don't want to give up *the actual sin*.

Remember Harold who came into my office and shared his problem with anger? His wife had threatened to leave him, and his children never stayed home when he was around because they both feared and resented his temper. He wanted his wife to stay, and he wanted a better relationship with his children. But he didn't want to give up his temper because he used it to control his family. He wanted me to teach him how to use his temper in a way that would not hurt his family. What a paradox!

Repentance

All these reactions to a troubled conscience keep us at an arm's length from God. God demands only one response when our conscience bothers us—to repent of our sin and then ask God's forgiveness.

What exactly is repentance? First, *a change of view.* I

admit that I sinned. I give up all excuses. Second, *a change of feelings*. I truly sorrow at my sin. I not only see the pain it caused others, but I realize that it offended God, assaulted his dignity, and this grieves me. Third, *a change of purpose*. The Greek word for *repentance* actually means to turn away from something. I turn my back on my sin, making a pledge to God not to sin like that again.

Repentance prepares the way for forgiveness. When I truly repent, then I ask God to forgive me—and he does. Many people struggle with this process. They feel a need to do more before God will forgive their sins. Yet God simply asks that we repent and ask his forgiveness.

He forgives our sin, not because of what we do, but because he promised to forgive. This promise is based on Jesus' life, death, and resurrection.

God gives us forgiveness as a gift. Surprised? We shouldn't be. Anyone who forgives us for doing wrong pays the penalty for our sin himself. And Jesus bore the heaviest penalty for all of our sins—by dying in agony on the cross.

"This sounds fine," you may respond, "but I still don't feel forgiven."

If you don't feel forgiven, put your thoughts on trial. "Have I repented?"

Yes.

"Has God promised to forgive when I repent?"

Yes.

"Am I then forgiven?"

Yes.

Then my feelings have no bearing on whether I'm forgiven. It may help to erect some material reminder of

God's forgiveness—a personal monument like a stake driven in the ground of your backyard. Or you might mark the date when you claimed a particular promise of God in the margin of your Bible. Then when you doubt God's forgiveness, you can go back to your "monument" and refresh your memory. Talk to yourself about how God forgives and fulfills his promises until your feelings change.

"What happens, though, when I sin again?" Look at the paradox. God calls us to a life of freedom from sin. "Be perfect even as your heavenly Father is perfect." Yet God says, "Confess your sin and I will forgive your sin." God realizes that we are human and we make mistakes. He is always willing to forgive us when we fail.

In *A Handbook of Concepts for Living,* Bill Bright examines what he calls *spiritual breathing.* By confessing our sins, we exhale the bad and useless from our lives. Then we re-commit our lives to Christ and inhale what is good and necessary for Christian living. Our lives are a cycle of exhaling the bad (sin) and inhaling the good (our renewed Christian commitment).

If you have carefully followed these instructions and still are troubled, seek out a mature Christian friend. In his/her presence, confess your sin to God. Then when you're in doubt, your friend can verbally remind you that you did confess your sin to God and that God has indeed forgiven you.

Asking Others for Forgiveness
God's forgiveness only solves part of the problem. If you have hurt others with your sin, you also need to ask their

forgiveness. But how? "That's not easy," you say.

Here are a few suggestions:

First, *arm yourself with the proper attitude—humility.* Just because you are asking another's forgiveness doesn't mean you are superior. In asking forgiveness you are doing nothing more than following God's instructions about righting past wrongs.

Second, *choose an appropriate time and place.* Don't ask for forgiveness when a person is preoccupied with something else or is emotionally overwrought. Seek privacy and freedom from interruptions.

I hurt a college professor once by excessively criticizing his teaching methods. We met one day on the road to campus. God had been speaking to me about my sin, so I walked up, ready to apologize. But he had been brooding on my offense. Before I could speak, he attacked. When he finished speaking, I apologized, but the words didn't sink in. His anger plugged his ears. A week later I straightened the matter out in private. That experience taught me a lot about proper timing.

I've found this simple progression in asking forgiveness helpful:

1. *"I was wrong."* Be brief. The other person can probably add many details you forgot long ago. Always be ready to listen to his side.

I once called a man to ask forgiveness for mistreating him five years earlier. When I apologized he commented, "Oh, it was nothing." But then he proceeded to recall the event with details I had long since forgotten.

2. *"Please forgive me."* Be honestly sorry and humble. Be patient and wait for the other person's reply.

Most people will respond, "Oh, that's all right." But it isn't. If it were, you wouldn't be feeling guilty or have to ask for forgiveness.

Asking another's forgiveness humbles us and gives backbone to our desire to change. It increases our determination not to sin like that again. However, if you do, ask forgiveness again. It's the only way to lick the problem.

3. If the person you have hurt is a family member or close friend, you need to add a third step: *"I love (care for) you."*

Reassure that person of your love, care, and concern. Explain briefly that he is important to you and that you wanted to clear the air to improve your relationship. Whether the other person chooses to forgive immediately or not is his choice. But at least the last words he will remember you saying will be positive self-builders. And warm fuzzies have a way of working their way into hearts and minds.

What if others won't forgive? Nothing we can do will ensure that another person will, indeed, forgive us. If you ask for forgiveness and receive refusal, you have done what you can. Don't send yourself on a guilt trip when the problem is now on the other person's side. However, remember that God still calls on you to love your neighbor as yourself.

Learning to Forgive Yourself

Let's look at this problem.

"I've asked for God's forgiveness a million times, but I never feel forgiven" you say. Usually we don't feel forgiven because we refuse to forgive ourselves.

Why?

How do we forgive ourselves?

First, we need to separate our feelings of shame and sorrow from our knowledge that we have asked for and received God's forgiveness. Even when fully forgiven, we may still feel sorrow and shame because we alienated others and violated God's and our own standards.

As a child I, along with my classmates, nicknamed a girl in our class "monkeyface." I still look back on the experience with sorrow and shame. As a counselor I know the damage we probably did in her life. I know God has forgiven me, but even now I still feel sorrow and shame whenever I think about it.

The way we feel from day to day does not depend on whether God forgives us or not. He has given us his forgiveness and cleared us of our burdensome pasts. If we carry our feelings of guilt into the present, *it is our choice*.

Forgiveness means that we express our sorrow in repentance instead of guilt. When others comment on our sins, we admit our sorrow, tell how God dealt with us, and move on into the future. Then God lifts the weight of our sinful pasts.

Sometimes we refuse to forgive ourselves. What we did is incredibly awful. When this happens, we can challenge our thinking with a question: "Am I a stricter judge than God?" If we answer "yes," our answer attacks God's judgment. In effect we are saying, "You, God, are mistaken in the way you're handling my sin. If you had my wisdom and insight, you'd never forgive me. Since you obviously aren't as wise as I, I'll continue to punish myself until you catch on and punish me yourself."

We accuse God of foolishness when we refuse to forgive ourselves.

What happens when God frees us from the chains of guilt? We feel freedom. A great burden lifts. Joy and buoyancy return to our lives. Life takes on a whole new meaning. We feel truly alive!

Things to Do/Think About:
1. Find a place where you won't be disturbed.
2. Ask God to forgive you for each unforgiven sin and then claim his promise of forgiveness.
3. Seek out one person you've hurt and ask his forgiveness.
4. Examine your heart and mind to make sure you've truly forgiven yourself.

For Further Reading:
Bill Bright, *A Handbook of Concepts for Living* (Here's Life)
David Seamands, *Healing for Damaged Emotions* (Victor)
Bernard Bangley, *Forgiving Yourself* (Harold Shaw)

8

I'm So Lonely
I Can't Stand It!

Please come as soon as you can, for Demas has left
me. He loved the good things of this life and went to
Thessalonica. Crescens has gone to Galatia, Titus to
Dalmatia. Only Luke is with me. Bring Mark with
you when you come, for I need him. (Tychicus is gone,
too, as I sent him to Ephesus.) When you come, be
sure to bring the coat I left at Troas with Brother
Carpus, and also the books, but especially the parch-
ments.

Alexander the coppersmith has done me much harm.
The Lord will punish him, but be careful of him, for he
fought against everything we said (2 Timothy 4:9-15).

DOES THIS PASSAGE give you a different picture
of the apostle Paul? He's a lonely old man, waiting in
prison for a judgment he knows means death. Most of

his friends have deserted him. Some have actually betrayed him while he was in prison, and we see his hurt at their betrayal. He begs Timothy to join him for the winter.

As a minister, I can understand Paul's feelings. Because loving, concerned Christians surround a minister, many people don't realize that he often gets lonely. Usually when a pastor meets with church people, whether socially, in church, or in counseling, he is *their minister,* and ministers usually get treated a bit differently from other people. Because of busy schedules, many pastors make few friends outside the church. But like everyone else, they need close friends and confidantes with whom they can share their personal burdens.

Loneliness—A Modern Problem

Loneliness permeates modern life. Why? For many different reasons. Sometimes false values make people lonely. For example, many people approach work as competition rather than cooperation. This means they don't work with each other to do a good job but rather to see who will be the best and earn the next promotion. When we help a fellow worker, we set the stage for that person to pass us. If we ask for help, we admit weakness. Promotions go to the strong, the self-sufficient.

Our image of the ideal home also creates loneliness. What is the ideal home? One that nestles back on a wooded lot of at least four acres. It's quiet, secluded, as far away from other houses as possible. If given the choice, who would pick a crowded apartment building over a large wooded estate and mansion? Whether we are poor, middle-class, or wealthy, our homes are our castles—forts where we can block out the noise and discomfort of the world outside. People often isolate themselves from one another on purpose when they choose their home.

And who lives in our ideal homes? Ideal persons—the independent, do-it-all-alone individuals who don't need anyone else. But they are also lonely, many times without close friends, living only for themselves. This self-suffi-cient image only compounds their loneliness. They know they can't stand alone, but they fear turning to others for a variety of reasons.

When Do I Get Lonely?

Loneliness gets more intense at key times in our life cycles. Many teens are lonely and insecure. They are at crossroads in their lives. Although they still act like chil-dren at times, they are becoming adults physically, emo-tionally, and intellectually. Many of them are struggling to find out who they really are and where they fit in the adult world. While they still need the affection and support of Mom and Dad, they wrestle to have freedom and inde-pendence. Even though they may talk for hours on the phone with a best friend and have lunch every day with a large group of friends, most teens will admit that they are lonely.

The mother of preschool children often suffers from loneliness. She loves her children, but they cannot talk about adult ideas and concerns. The children keep her too busy to work part-time or to have lunch with her single friends very often. Finances may keep her tied down, too. She may have to struggle to make a dinner that isn't hamburger or macaroni again. Even when she snatches time for herself (that precious hour in the bubble bath!), she's too worn out to enjoy it. She begins to feel cooped up and alone.

Who else suffers from loneliness? The twenty-five to forty-five-year-old man. Maybe his job moves him from his hometown to a strange community. He struggles to develop his career potential, tries to start a family, takes on a large mortgage, all with less money and experience than at any time in his life. Because his peers share his struggles, no one has time or energy left to help anyone else. In today's mobile society, he may not even stay in the community long enough to make good friends.

The final cycle of life creates painful loneliness as friends and family are lost. A spouse, a brother, sister, or close friend may die. Children live their own lives. Physical disabilities make it more and more difficult to visit the friends who remain. Finances are often tight. Widows and widowers admit that loneliness is incredibly hard to fight.

The Masks of Loneliness
If we only knew *when* we were lonely, we could fight it. But loneliness wears many masks. It makes us feel like something is missing from our lives. When a spouse dies, we can readily point to a reason for our loneliness, but often we feel nothing specific—just a void. Sometimes a close examination of our lives helps us discover, "I have no one I can call a close friend." Other times we are so close to our own situation that someone else will have to point out the problem.

When you are lonely, you may feel that nobody understands. Of course each experience we have is unique—God created each of us differently. But by sharing our experiences with each other we can learn to uplift each other. We may discover that a special friend or friends makes us feel less lonely.

Harry was a special friend. For three years he pastored the Baptist church across town. We met often to discuss common problems in ministry. Then Harry moved. Since then, I have never developed the special relationship with another minister that I had with Harry. And in times of pastoral stress, I feel lonely. I miss his companionship and concern for me. I miss the times we prayed together and wonder if I will ever find another friend like Harry—someone with whom I had so much in common.

Feeling rejected and deserted also contributes to loneliness. We may cry inside for others to be near, to telephone or drop by, but no one does. When a spouse dies, family and friends rush in, but afterwards everyone goes their own way and seems to forget, although that is the time when we need their support the most.

Another mask of loneliness is insecurity. We worry, "If something bad should happen, no one would know, no one would help!" For three years my wife attended school 100 miles away for three days a week. Occasionally as I came home to meet the children after school I thought, "What would they do if she did not show up one evening?" I was afraid for my children and for myself. The more I considered this possibility, the more anxious and unnerved I became until I learned to put her in God's hands.

When we feel lonely, we often feel anxious, restless,

tense. We may pace the house, wondering what's wrong with us. We search for things to keep us busy, but nothing seems to work. We try to fill a void with *things* when only another *person* can meet our need.

When we feel lonely, we feel hopeless, trapped in a situation we can't change. The future is not simply bleak— it is gone, but we have to keep on living. We are sure things will never change, but we have to keep on going.

We often complicate this with feelings of worthlessness. In a society that values people for achievements, we question our worth. Each of us does this sometime in our lives. Maybe you feel worthless because you're just an average student and not a straight "A" achiever, an average housekeeper and not a superwoman, or an average worker and not a manager. Or maybe you get discouraged watching the perfect people on TV when you haven't lost a pound after holding to a rigorous diet for the last six weeks. You begin to feel worthless, unloved, unlovable, lonely.

What does all this lead to? *Depression.* And the vicious cycle repeats itself. The feeling that something important is missing from our lives makes us depressed, deepening our loneliness. This loneliness in turn makes us more depressed.

While loneliness hurts by itself, it also complicates our lives. Lonely people often do strange or foolish things. They go to bars to be with other people and around activity and drink too much so they can escape the loneliness they feel. They telephone the weatherman just to hear an adult voice. They sleep around with many partners because they want to be close to someone, but then they feel lonelier. Many lonely people also let others take advantage of them because they so desperately need company, for good or bad.

Loneliness makes holidays and special occasions difficult. We end up measuring the holidays by who is missing instead of enjoying what we have. And then joy is replaced by sorrow.

Sometimes loneliness even hurts physically as well as psychologically. It both creates and feeds on negative attitudes, creating an ever downward cycle. Lonely people sometimes find themselves reaching up to touch bottom.

How Not to Fight Loneliness

People fight loneliness with many weapons. First, let's take a look at a few that don't work.

Some live a hectic social life. I advise our local Parents Without Partners. Single parents amaze me with their social schedules. Many run from loneliness with endless activity. Sometimes it works, but most often it makes a bad situation worse. When their social time ends, the loneliness hits many even harder when they realize that they need close friends desperately.

People also fight loneliness by withdrawing into passive activities. They come home and turn on the TV for companionship, or just to escape and become someone else for a while. Other people use books, solitaire, or even church activities.

Others fight loneliness by trying to be with people constantly. Julie told me, "After my divorce I visited my brother Larry and his family a lot."

But being with others doesn't relieve loneliness permanently. She confessed, "One time we sat there enjoying ourselves when I was suddenly overwhelmed with a desperate feeling of loneliness. The togetherness of their family just made it worse. I quickly stood up and ran into the bathroom where I had a good cry."

Thinking about the past can also make you lonely. Joan is a good example. "About a year after John died, I sold the double bed," she related. "I just got all torn up looking at it, crawling into it by myself each night."

Hiding Loneliness

Loneliness seems so common. Apart from depression, it probably afflicts more people than any other emotional problem. So why don't we admit our loneliness and deal with it?

Through TV, movies, and advertising, our society says, "Lonely people are failures." Who wants to admit failure? Society says strong independent people don't need others. If I admit I'm lonely, I'm also admitting, "I need others." And then society responds, "Something is wrong with you. You're weak."

Our society also declares, "Successful, important, worthwhile people have many friends. They always have people around them." However, this view denies the importance of creative solitude, a necessity to becoming important or successful.

Finally, society demands a quick adjustment to major loss, like a loved one's death. In general, people who have not been bereaved are the ones who urge others to "get back to living, forget about the past. Live for now." Grieving, however, may take one, two, or many years. A chance remark or an unexpected memory can overwhelm us with grief years later.

My father died four years ago. This past week as I drove near my childhood home, my thoughts turned to the times we spent together. My eyes welled up with tears as I realized that those times are past.

Society denies these feelings, making us feel isolated and alone. And as part of our society, we share its general views and condemn ourselves for loneliness. As a result we deny or try to hide our loneliness. We don't even admit to ourselves our need for close companionship. But hiding and denial only compounds our problems.

Overcoming Loneliness

How do we overcome loneliness? Let's begin by distinguishing *loneliness* from *aloneness*. There's a great deal of difference. As a writer I deeply value alone time because I can focus all my thoughts without any interruption. I never feel lonely when I am alone and writing. It's my time to *choose* aloneness.

But when events *force* aloneness on me, that's different. Loneliness may have nothing to do with being alone. I've walked the crowded streets of Chicago at noon, knowing that if I suddenly disappeared from the sidewalk, no one would even notice. You can be acutely lonely when surrounded by people—simply ask the person who spent a few months or even years in a loveless marriage, knowing divorce would come eventually.

Earlier in this chapter we talked about the many masks of loneliness. Many people, struggling with loneliness, can't put their finger on what is wrong. But when we do recognize the symptoms of loneliness, we should admit that we need others.

Is loneliness a sin or the direct result of sin? No, not in itself. However it is the result of our sinful state and the accumulation of sin in our lives.

Adam and Eve sensed shame and nakedness the moment they sinned. Nothing makes us more alone than shame. We all hide past sins we don't want others to know about. These hidden sins separate us from others, making us feel lonely. Loneliness is as detrimental to human life as death and sickness. Until Christ returns, we will all battle loneliness.

How can we combat our loneliness? By attacking rather than reacting. Many of us give in to our loneliness until we wallow in the pits. We need to act offensively instead of defensively. We need to attack loneliness before it attacks us.

Let's look at a few practical solutions.

First, *plan "alone times."* Loneliness troubles many people because they are afraid to be (or don't know how to be) alone. By planning "alone times" we teach ourselves to face aloneness. Make the first ones short—half an hour. As you learn how to use "alone times," you will take your first step in dealing with loneliness.

Second, *plan to use "alone times" for personal growth.* We all complain about lack of time to do all the things we want to do. Plan to use "alone time" to get involved in those things. Work on your spiritual growth, too. Develop your relationship with Jesus Christ through Bible reading, study, and memorization. Learn about your faith by reading books that encourage growth, that give Bible background, that teach church history, that improve your ministry skills. Make "alone times" productive.

Third, *develop friendships*. Nothing overcomes loneliness like friendship. I'm in the twenty-five to forty-five-year-old range—documented to be one of the loneliest periods in the life cycles of men. We also live far from the rest of our family. When loneliness wears me down, I call someone and do something active with him. I used to wait for others to call me, but I discovered how important taking the initiative is in making friends.

Remember, when you feel lonely, someone else does too. They may be sitting at home waiting for the telephone to ring, for a friend to say, "Let's get together." Some people are shy and feel awkward making the initial move. Others lead hectic lives and feel they don't have time. And others may be just plain lazy. Do you fit into any of the categories? If you are lonely, take the initiative. Who knows? Maybe someone's waiting for you!

Fourth, *anticipate bad times and plan for them*. Many people feel lonely at holidays. Others struggle with special family occasions. Sunday afternoons and evenings are terribly lonely for college students and many widows and widowers. Plan to spend time with someone when you know you'll be feeling lonely.

Finally, *beat loneliness by reaching out to serve others*— not only friends and acquaintances, but those you don't know. As the force of working women increases, the number of volunteers diminishes. Many organizations cry for volunteers to meet important people needs. Look around for something you would like to do, then volunteer. People will greet you with open arms. While you're help-

ing others, you'll overcome your own loneliness. And that
is indeed triumph!

Things to Do/Think About:
1. At what times are you lonely?
2. Plan an "alone time." Write down what you are going to do during that
   time.
3. How well did it work? Were you lonely? Why or why not?
4. Take the initiative. Call someone the next time you feel lonely.

9

I'm Supposed to Be Perfect (So What's Wrong with Me?)

GOD DELIGHTS IN YOU, just as you are.

"Are you kidding?" you say.

Do you really believe that God accepts and loves you just as you are? Most people don't. They react inwardly and say, "No, you're wrong. God doesn't like me as I am. He wants me to be better. He wants me to love him more. He wants me to do his will more. He certainly isn't delighted with (insert an area of frequent temptation or failure)."

Why do we feel this way about God?

Many view God as an unpleasable parent. Remember when you brought that special report card home from school? You never claimed to be a top student, but this time you tried especially hard to please Mom and Dad. You received all *A*s except for one *B*. Well, Mom took one look and said, "Why did you get a *B?* What's wrong with you? I know you can get all *A*s."

Crestfallen but determined, you worked like never before in your life—no television, no radio, less time with your friends. It showed in a straight *A* report card. You burst the buttons on your shirt as you handed your parents your report card. Your father looked at it without comment and then said, "How come you got your shoes wet coming home from school?"

You wondered, "Can I ever do enough to satisfy them?"

Many Christians live by the unspoken philosophy, "Only perfection satisfies God. When I'm perfect, God will accept me."

Most of us present God with our best sides when we pray. Strange, isn't it? Especially when God knows everything about us. Why should we pretend with him? Maybe we think he will reject us if we expose our bad sides. When you pray, do you let God see the real you with all your faults and hangups?

We strive for perfection. In all situations we want to please God, ourselves, and others—perfectly. But such thinking strips the joy from life and stunts our growth and development as persons and as Christians.

What Is Perfectionism?

In *Healing for Damaged Emotions,* David Seamands has a lot to say on the subject. A perfectionist lives by the tyranny of the oughts. His self-talk says, "I could have . . ." "I should have . . ." "If only I would have . . ." A perfectionist always falls short of the standards he sets for himself. He always points out the little thing that went wrong. He remains convinced that the next time he will do better. Yet he never quite pleases himself no matter what he does.

A perfectionist always feels guilty about something. Because he lives by unrealistic standards, he will always fall short of his own expectations. Thus he is always a failure in his own eyes.

He compounds this problem by thinking in all-or-nothing categories. Most people are satisfied when a project is 75% or 83% or 95% perfect. The perfectionist uses one grading system—either 100% or 0%. By thinking this way, he sets himself up for failure and its resulting guilt.

The second characteristic grows out of the first. *Perfectionists live with anxiety because of the tyranny of the oughts.*

I enjoy a crazy sport—ice fishing. As fall progresses toward winter, my anticipation grows. When the first ice freezes, I'm the first one out on it. That creates problems. How safe is the first ice? To protect myself against a cold bath, I wear a life preserver and fish with a buddy. As I fish, my gut tightens with each crack of the ice. A perfectionist feels that way much of the time. He waits for the ice to break and suck him and his world through a big hole into the black void beyond.

Third, *a perfectionist lives by rigid, overly strict, moral standards.* He follows biblical standards with Pharisaic precision and creates his own personal fences around the law to keep himself from violating God's will. He invests the fences with the same moral value as the biblical command, creating even more pressure to live by an impossible standard.

He never gives up, though, because his standard, whether conscious or unconscious, protects his fragile self-esteem. Some perfectionists feel that their rigid standards earn brownie points with God. Although salvation is by faith, the perfectionist struggles day-in, day-out to earn God's favor and others' approval. His super-strict moral code is his primary tool.

Problems develop. The more he judges himself by his over-strict code, the more he begins judging others by the same code. He assumes they are failing God when they don't measure up to his code, even when their living conforms to biblical standards.

Perfectionists use self-deprecation to hide their low self-esteem. They cut themselves down because they feel that God doesn't accept them. To forestall criticism from others for his obvious failures, the perfectionist heaps it on himself. He beats everyone else to the punch. Then others feel trapped into complimenting him because they feel he is continually cutting himself down.

Perfectionists also complicate their lives by an over-developed need to please others. The hyper-sensitivity of a perfectionist to criticism sometimes leads to ridiculous behavior.

We can't please everyone. It's an impossible task. Sometimes the more we try to please, the more we feel we fail. And that makes us angry—at others and ourselves.

Anger frequently dominates a perfectionist, whether he knows it or not. In marriage counseling I administer a test that exposes hidden anger. When I tell a person, "the test says that you're quite angry," I often get a vehement denial. I then say, "Anger takes two forms. Many people's anger explodes like a bomb. Others hide their anger inside, frequently directing their anger largely at themselves. Could this be the form anger takes in your life?"

They often think a moment, then quietly say, "I never thought about it like that. Yes, I'm very angry—inside."

Why? You may feel that others mistreat you, take advantage of you, never show appreciation, let you do all the dirty work, and so on.

How do you handle those feelings? By directing your anger at yourself? Maybe you think you don't meet life's challenges as well as others do, or that things never go right for you ("If only . . ."). You hate your shortcomings and failures.

Are you angry at God because you think he's shortchanged you? That he gave others greater talents and more advantages, better parents, better families? Or that he gave you a raw deal when he let some tragedy happen?

If you feel angry much of the time, you may be a perfectionist. Being hard on yourself won't help you or any situation in your life. And the anger you carry over to God will prevent you from seeing him in a biblical perspective. Satan loves to use anger as a foothold on you.

You may try to hide your anger so others won't know

about it. You may fear what will happen if you show just how angry you are at life and its injustices. Many "nice, quiet, easy-going" people are lit powder kegs, just waiting for the right moment to explode.

Why Choose Perfectionism?

Why are there so many perfectionists when perfectionism burdens us with an unbearable load? Perfectionists frequently grow up in homes with demanding parents. They feel that no matter what they do, no matter how hard they try, their parents ask for more. No effort, no matter how diligent, satisfies them. As adults, they keep on trying to please their unpleasable parents.

After the "Hands Across America" fund drive, the organizer was asked, "Why did you do this?"

He laughed as he replied, "I guess I did it to please my parents. I know that sounds stupid, since I'm forty-seven, but I want to please them, to give them something to be proud of."

Perfectionists often grow up in homes with an unpredictable atmosphere. When they sit down for dinner they never know whether they will be praised or berated. And even worse, they never know why they will receive praise or blame. When they were children, sometimes Dad would spend hours playing with them when they asked. Other times he would explode in anger. They could never anticipate their parents' reactions. Today through trial and error, they have chosen perfectionism—hoping that it will bring success where other means have failed.

Finally, perfectionists often carry deep, unforgiven pain from the past. They remember childhood hurts in photographic detail, with precise memories of who was there and what was said. Many of us live with shameful childhood memories of times we mistreated other children. Some of those children, now adults, still ache with unbearable pain because of the way they were treated.

Most perfectionists hide their anger inside when they think about these events. Occasionally their rage slips out. Something mildly upsetting happens, yet they react with rage. Even if they don't realize it, someone reached back into their past and touched an open wound they thought was bandaged.

Overcoming Perfectionism

How can you break free from the bondage of perfectionism?

Remember that God loves you just as much when you fail as when you succeed. Romans 8:1 says, "There is now no condemnation awaiting those who belong to Christ Jesus." By freeing us from the threat of judgment, God assures us that he loves us, even when we fail.

God does not base his love on our character. He gives us his love as a gift. How does a person become a child of God? By faith, through God's grace, apart from works. This teaching sets Christianity apart from all other religions. Faith excludes any good works on our part to gain God's favor. If we ask, God freely, through grace, gives us salvation as an unmerited gift.

Once God makes us his children, how do we remain his children? By working our tails off to please him? Of course not! We remain his children in the same way we became his children—through grace, apart from works.

Why? Because God knows we cannot earn the right of being his child even after Christ is our Savior. If our status depended on perfect obedience, we would be kicked out of God's family within minutes of accepting Jesus as Savior. Every day, many times each day, we would have to be re-converted.

Our behavior, then, does nothing to change our standing with God. He loves us just as much when we fail as when we perfectly obey him.

"How can that be?" some exclaim in astonishment.

I have three sons. Many times when they were two or three, they would come running into the house when we had company and rush to the family bathroom. A few minutes later they'd come out, pants down, and ask for help.

Let's judge their behavior for a moment by adult standards. What would people do to me if I charged into mixed company with my pants down? I would be thrown into jail or committed to a mental hospital.

When children do the same thing, we take them from the room, explain the need for modesty, and send them on their way. Why the difference? Children are immature.

God recognizes his children's immaturity—immaturity that often leads them into sinful behavior. But as their loving heavenly Father, he responds not so much to their sin as to their need to mature. As they mature, they should sin less and less. Their many failures on the road to maturity do not revoke their status as his children. He loves his children just as much in their immaturity and failure as he does in their growth toward maturity.

God loves us as much on the day of our conversion as

on the day of our perfection when we are transformed into his likeness in heaven. He does not base his love on what we do, but on who he is, our loving heavenly Father. By loving us no matter what, he frees us from the burden of living in fear of his wrath so we can enjoy living with a God who unconditionally loves us.

Some Practical Suggestions

Here are some suggestions for challenging perfectionistic self-talk.

When you tell yourself, "I ought to . . ." or "I should . . ." ask this question, "What happens if I fail?"

Don't make a catastrophe out of every mistake. If you fail, then what? Surprisingly, most people won't even notice. If they do, they won't care. Why? Because they know you make mistakes, but they love you anyway. Cling to this thought in the face of failure, "Even when I fail, God still loves me." In the end, nothing else really matters.

Let's go further. To learn what happens when you fail, plan a few small failures. This may sound crazy, but try it. What happens? Most people won't even notice. If they do, correct your mistake. Failure isn't such a big thing as we make it out to be.

Until about eight years ago, I lived in constant fear of failure. In each church I served, I feared failure, so I tried to do far more than people expected, trying to reach perfection in everything. I practically memorized each sermon before I preached. Then a church fired me. And my biggest single failure turned into my most liberating experience. While failure hurt, I learned that I can still enjoy life. God still loves me. My family and friends still love me. I can serve God well in other ways and places. Failure isn't such a big deal after all.

When you catch yourself saying, "I ought to . . ." challenge yourself with "Who says?" What authority stands behind this "ought?"

Megan and her husband Jim were already leading the teen group at their church, organizing a college/career group Bible study at their home during the week, and doing music for the morning service every few weeks. One Sunday a deaconess walked up to Megan and said, "You really should take your turn on the deaconesses' board this year. May I sign you up?"

Megan was quiet for a few minutes, her stomach churning. She and Jim both had jobs that took forty hours out of their week, in addition to the time they took for church ministries. They hardly had any time for each other. Yet every time someone asked her to do something else she told herself, "I really ought to. After all, it's for God." As a child, she was told that ministering for God was the most important thing in life. And yet, she wondered, "Why can't someone else do it? Jim and I are doing so much already!"

Megan is an example of a perfectionist. Growing up under strict parental rules, she feels she has to be a super-woman for God. She needs to challenge her self-made, "I ought to's" with "Who says?" When she realizes that she is the one pushing herself to live up to an unreasonable standard, it will be easier to say no.

Challenge your self-made oughts with "Who says?" When you first violate some of your "oughts" that are unnecessarily restricting your joy in life (this does not include spiritual commandments for right living set up by Jesus' example), you will feel uncomfortable. As your conscience grows, those feelings of guilt will grow less and less.

Perfectionists often judge their actions by two categories—absolute perfection or complete failure.

You can beat this kind of all-or-nothing way of thinking by giving yourself permission to earn less than 100 percent on a few tasks. Under the first suggestion for challenging perfectionistic self-talk, we looked at what happens when we plan a total failure. But what happens if we do an eighty-percent job?

Plan to do an eighty-percent job tomorrow and look at the results. Most people won't notice the difference. The few that comment will probably say, "It's nice to see you decided to live by normal human standards at last." Trying to do and be 100 percent in everything is a killer—mentally and spiritually. Just try to do what you can in the time you have.

Finally, *challenge your fear, "What will people think?"*

Perfectionists live in fear of others' condemnation. Ask yourself honestly, "What if they don't like me? What will happen?" If others reject me, God still loves me because he never rejects his children. If some don't like me, others will.

Sometimes when I've been rejected, I say to myself, "If they don't like me, it's their problem." Sound egotistical? In some ways. But in other ways it isn't.

When a person rejects me for doing something I enjoy (that is not sinful), they are telling me, "If you will be someone else, I'll like you." How utterly unfair! Quite

frankly, if you spend much of your life trying to be someone else to earn your friends' and acquaintances' favor,
then you all need new friends.

This seems like a harsh statement, but I'm beginning
to believe it. You must be able to be *who you are* with
your friends. If you can't, look at yourself and your relationships closely. Be considerate. Take into account your
own and others' needs. Don't excuse sinful behavior by
saying, "That's just the way I am. Take it or leave it."
Remember that the most important thing is seeking to
live the best life you can for Jesus Christ.

When you have this attitude, you're declaring, "God
alone judges my life." I want to please him. This means
I try to love others as myself. If others reject my lifestyle
and as a result reject me, I fall back on the fact that God
alone judges my life. I live and die to him and to him
alone.

Gaining freedom from perfectionism generates unbelievable peace and rest. When we glory in God's uncondi-
tional love, he gives freedom. Wallow in that love. Learn
to relax in what he's done and *is doing* for you.

One caution—remember we don't change overnight.
Gaining freedom from perfectionism takes time and effort. As you implement what was shared in this chapter
with prayer and an honest desire to change, God will free
you from this burden, step by step.

Things to Do/Think About:
1. Memorize Romans 8:1 in a modern translation as a reminder of your
   freedom from judgment.
2. Write out three "oughts" that control your life.
3. Write out at least two challenges for each your "oughts."

4. Plan a few eighty-percent jobs and examine the results of your "failure."

For Further Reading:
David Seamands, *Healing for Damaged Emotions* (Victor Books)

10

Will the Real Me Please Stand Up?

SUSIE WAS EXCITED to see Alice. She raced up to her, exclaiming, "Guess what? I've got the pictures from your shower last week. Do you want to see them?"

Alice grabbed the pictures and tore open the envelope. She glanced through them quickly with a comment here and there. Suddenly she held up a picture for Susie and said, "That sure doesn't look like me!"

Of course, both of them knew the picture was indeed of Alice. But she was talking about something else. Each of us has a picture inside our heads we call "ME." When a picture taken with a camera does not agree with our inner picture, we reject it by saying, "That's just not me."

What we're saying is that the photograph violates our inner picture—something about it just doesn't square with what we think of ourselves.

How do we develop this inner picture? As a growing child your family made comments about you. As you heard these comments you filed them under "ME," slowly but surely creating a picture of who you are. When you took a drawing to your mother and she said, "Why, honey, that's a nice picture. Can you draw me another one?" she was saying you had talent as an artist. As a result you practiced more at drawing and became more talented in that area. Under "ME" you placed a file folder labeled "Artist" where you collected "artist comments."

But when you lifted your voice in song, and she yelled, "Hey, would you kids quit teasing the cat!" you also filed that statement. In the future you chose to sing where no one else could hear you. This file folder filled with negative comments.

Many different events like these went together (and still are accumulating) to create the picture you have in your mind labeled "ME." This picture determines how much you value yourself.

What Makes a Positive Self-Image?

The Holy Spirit planted four basic emotional needs in each of us. And when those are met, our self-image increases in positive leaps and bounds. Let's take a closer look at them.

1. *We need to be loved or to belong to a group we think is significant.* Much of this need should be cared for in our family life, but for many people this need goes unmet.

When that happens we seek substitutes. And the substitute for love is *attention*.

Three-year-old Peter is a good example. Every time you turn around, little Peter is there asking you to do something with him. Finally, in frustration, you yell, "Please leave me alone. Can't you see I have to get ready for our company tonight?"

Peter slowly drags away. Suddenly you realize the house has become strangely quiet. Peter hasn't bothered you for half an hour. Now you're ready to give him all your attention because you wonder what he's up to. You slip quietly down the hall and open the door to his room. As you peek in, you see him contentedly drawing pictures on the wall with a red crayon. When you didn't give him love he sought attention, and now you are really going to give him some!

Adults react much the same when love is withdrawn from them. The adult who seeks attention is one who always has a joke to tell, who dominates every conversation, whose story is just a little bit better than the other guy's, who shows up to a meeting a few minutes late so people will notice him, who drinks excessively. We can list many different things, all pointing to the need for attention. Here is a person who wants to be loved. But when he can't be loved, he seeks attention.

2. *We need to be confident of ourselves.* Confidence comes from knowing there are things in life we do well. It doesn't really matter whether it's repairing a car, writing a book, or creating a gourmet meal. What we need to know is that we can do some things well. Then we feel good about ourselves.

However, our need for confidence is not met when we respond in one of two ways. One is when *we seek power and control over others*. We dominate the meetings we attend, we seek elected offices or positions over others.

Some of us, however, don't have the personality for this. How do we respond?

We defy any authority other than our own. This can be done either through active challenge or passive resistance. We decide that no one can tell us what to do. We are our own bosses. But underneath it all, all we really want is confidence in ourselves.

3. *We need to feel we have worth or value.* This means that we not only have confidence that comes from doing a job well, but also that we are doing something important. Our value and worth comes from *what we do* and *who we're doing things for.* We need to think we're significant, that when we aren't around, we're missed.

When this need is not met, we substitute performance and perfectionism. We make sure what we're doing is the best we can possibly do. But some of us go overboard in saying to people, "Look at what I can do." Our house is spotless, our car is in perfect mechanical condition, our clothes are the latest style, our makeup is just right. We're afraid to let people see that we might do or be less than the best.

So what do we do?

Try to cover it up when we feel that we are lacking in worth and value.

4. *We need to feel secure.* This is one reason why children from divorced homes have a hard time entering close relationships as they get older. They discovered early in

life that this world is not secure, at least not from their point of view. When we feel insecure, we naturally flee to what we think is safety. This may mean never having a different opinion from others—at least not expressing it when we do. We may be scared to take risks, or we may hold back from relationships with others because we might be rejected. We think we can find security by being milquetoast in many areas of our lives.

What Makes a Poor Self-Image?
Many of us have poor self-images. Why?

First, because *we judge our lives by worldly standards*. The cosmetic industry makes millions by telling us that if we look better than other people, we're acceptable. And if we're "sexy" enough and wear the right perfume, we'll attract the best specimens of men and women as friends. Many of us judge ourselves "inadequate" because we don't measure up to American standards of beauty.

The world also tells us we're acceptable if we achieve more than others—if we make the final touchdown that wins the game, own a Porsche, or have a home in the country. It doesn't really matter what the achievement is. We may be able to stack dominoes higher than anyone else. No matter how we strive for achievement, we're still trying to gain recognition from a world that says we're only worth having around if we achieve.

This world also tells us it will accept us if we hold a position of status—the mayor of a city, the only woman on the church staff, or the president of a large company. What matters is that we hold a position this world considers important. Others have to acknowledge our existence.

Can you measure up to these standards? I certainly can't. Most people never do. And the result is that most of us think poorly of ourselves. Each time we fail to measure up, our self-images take another nose-dive.

A poor self-image also comes from misinterpreting aspects of Christian teaching. Christians are acutely aware of their sinful condition. The Bible tells us that each of us is a sinner and that God condemns sinners. Many people draw the false conclusion from this, "Therefore I am worthless."

But that's not so! While I may be a sinner, if I have asked God into my heart and life, I'm also his redeemed child, created in his image. I'm anything but worthless. God delights in his children and gives them ultimate value.

Christians also confuse self-love, a key element in a positive self-image, with pride. Obviously, the Bible condemns pride, for it says pride is the root of all sin. Pride led Adam and Eve to challenge God in the Garden of Eden and to eat from the forbidden tree. But pride and self-love are two different things.

Unlike pride, self-love is humble. Humility means that you know who you are, but you willingly submit all you are to God's rule. You know your talents and abilities, accepting them without pride as a gift from God, and commit them to the Holy Spirit's direction. You can both love yourself and be perfectly humble because you're submitting who you are to God's rule.

Pride is the opposite. Pride is clinging to what you are and have, attempting to minimize its value so you can keep it—all the while refusing to do what God wants you to do.

The experiences of childhood and the teen years also tend to develop a poor self-image. Imagine for a moment the world from a child's perspective. Everyone around you is 15-20 feet tall, weighing about 750-1,000 pounds. They all have I.Q.'s above 200, the athletic ability of a professional, and the manual dexterity of a juggler. Every time you have trouble doing something, they can do it. Anytime something is too big for you to handle, they can handle it. Anytime you can't figure out a problem, they can.

Imagine how you would feel after living in that environment? Young people tend to feel that they will never reach these levels. And combined with the pressures of the teen years to be like everyone else, it gets harder and harder to maintain a healthy self-image.

Most of us interpret others' opinions about our lives with too much imagination and seriousness. When someone overlooks us, we think they hate us. When we're chosen last for a game, we think we're the worst athlete in the world. When we fail a single test, we conclude we're going to flunk the whole year. And because most of these fears are private, no one ever corrects them.

We also take too seriously others' criticisms.

Harriet was standing by the hot dog stand at the zoo when three ten-year-olds walked past. One of them commented to the others, "Have you ever seen anything uglier?"

Harriet turned to her friend and said, "See, even they know how ugly I am."

Much of our self-image then is based on childhood experiences and never examined by adult logic. We heard and experienced things as a child that gave us a negative image of ourselves. We continue to live with that image because we've never subjected it to realistic examination. If we would only reach out and try to overcome some of these barriers, we'd be astonished at what surfaces.

As Dan grew up, he was never encouraged to sing. In fact, he was actively discouraged. Then he married a skilled musician who commented on the quality of his voice. At first they practiced alone at home because he was afraid to sing in public, but eventually she persuaded him to try an easy solo in their small country church. He was astonished at people's responses. They enjoyed it. Slowly his adult logic enabled him to overcome his childhood feelings about his singing.

All of this wouldn't be so bad if we would only hear *every* evaluation of our lives. But we all have built-in filters that eliminate information that contradicts our self-image. If Fred stops by as you're building a patio porch on the back of the house and comments, "Boy, you're really going at it. And it looks great! Who says you've got two left thumbs when it comes to carpentry?"

Immediately you back off, discounting what he says, "Are you kidding? Fred can't even hammer a nail straight. His opinion doesn't count," and you go back to your image of yourself as a poor carpenter.

On the other hand if someone approaches you with a joking comment about your patio, "Oops, it looks like it's leaning about three feet to the left. And the stairs don't meet. In a few years when you're a grandpa, you won't even be able to balance yourself to climb them. Why don't you get a professional to do it?" you will remember that because it fits your image of yourself.

Our filters only let us accept comments that are consistent with what we already believe about ourselves unless someone makes a concentrated effort to break through or we make a concentrated effort to break out.

Enemies of Self-Esteem

While each of the factors we just discussed contributes to our poor self-image, certain basic attitudes toward life support a poor self-image.

1. *We believe that acceptance from God and others must be earned.* It's not surprising we think this way. While growing up, most children experience the rejection that comes when Mother says, "I don't like you when you do that." Even if she never says it, we soon learn that we are liked when we do good and rejected when we don't. On entering school we learn that the same standards apply. Most teachers like children who behave and reject children who don't.

Christian teaching *should* overcome our acceptance of this standard, but with most people it only partially succeeds. We all know that we come to Christ by faith, that salvation is a gift of God that we cannot earn by anything we do.

However after we are accepted as God's children, we spend the remainder of our lives trying to earn his favor. All the while the Holy Spirit stands beside us saying, "You're my child. What more can I make you?" But we're working so hard to earn his favor that his words rarely sink in. We need to learn that not only do we come to Christ by faith, but that we also live by faith. We are at all times accepted by God on the basis of Jesus' work at Calvary.

2. *We believe that all failures deserve to be punished.* Whenever we do something wrong, we believe someone should punish us. When no one is there, we often do the job ourselves. Nonetheless, God accepts us as we are— failures, goofs, and all. The beauty of Jesus' work is that he has already born all our punishment on the cross. There's nothing more that needs to be done. We only have to accept his finished work and enjoy our relationship with him. If God loved us while we were still rebelling against his will, how much more must he love us as his children?

3. *We believe that we should always live up to our own wishes and ideals.* Our lives are dominated by an impossible series of "shoulds" and "oughts," many having nothing to do with morality. As a result we berate ourselves for being less than we think we should be. *Yet God accepts us as we are and plans to help us become what he wants us to be.* When we don't live up to our ideals, he is not going to jump on us and tell us how horrible we are. Rather he picks us up, sets us on our feet, and helps us on our way again. He continues to accept us even when we fall short of our own ideals.

4. *We believe that we know best what will meet our own needs and make us happy.* This is the great American fallacy. "No one knows better than I what I need to meet my needs and, as a result, to make me happy." So we spend great amounts of time, energy, and money searching for ways to meet our own needs and gain happiness. All the while God, our heavenly Father, gives us what is best

for us and pours out one blessing after another. But we're unhappy because we aren't getting *what we think we need.* Our self-esteem suffers as a result.

Biblical Self-Image

What then is the biblical basis for a positive self-image? It stands on two pillars.

First, *I am a special creation of the all-wise, all-powerful God.* In Psalm 139:13-16 David shares, "You made all the delicate, inner parts of my body, and knit them together in my mother's womb. Thank you for making me so wonderfully complex! It is amazing to think about. Your workmanship is marvelous—and how well I know it. You were there while I was being formed in utter seclusion! You saw me before I was born and scheduled each day of my life before I began to breathe. Every day was recorded in your Book!"

The Holy Spirit was involved in our creation even while we were yet unborn. He oversaw our development, making sure each organ and each talent came out just the way he wanted. Therefore you are valuable because God created you unique.

Your value resides not in who you are in yourself, or in who others try to make you, but in the fact that you are God's handiwork.

This also means the Holy Spirit gave each of us individual talents to use and develop for his service. I have confidence because I know the Holy Spirit is using my talents to help others. While I may on occasion struggle to develop my talents, my confidence comes not through my perfect ability to use them but through my knowledge that the Holy Spirit gave me just the right level of talent to do the job he's asked me to do. My confidence again comes from him, not through any personal achievement.

The second pillar is that *I'm redeemed and adopted into God's family.* Romans 8 gives this story in detail. It tells me I can experience no greater love than that shown at the cross where God made it possible for me to belong by entering his family (31). He then adopted me to demonstrate to the world what he can do in and through a sinner such as me (15-16). I'm loved and secure because of who he is (29-30). It's not how hard I can cling to him, but the fact that he holds me in his hand that is the basis for my feelings (35-39). As a result I can feel good about myself because I know God.

What does this mean? In my relationship with Jesus Christ all my basic needs are met. Once I come to him I can rest in what he has done for me, knowing that he meets all my needs. My self-image, then, is a positive one because it's based on a relationship where the Holy Spirit constantly initiates the positive things happening in my life.

God's call for each of us is to live out our roles as created and redeemed by him. When we seek to live out these roles, then we can feel good about ourselves, not because we've attained some false standard, but because of *who we are and are becoming* through the Holy Spirit's work inside us.

Things to Do/Think About:
1. Which of the four basic emotional needs is not being met in your life?
2. Look back at the section on "What Makes a Poor Self-Image?" Do any of the reasons apply to you? Which ones?

3. Write down an example from your own life where each of the reasons you just listed plays a role in your self-image.
4. Review the four enemies of self-esteem. How do they affect your life?
5. Thank God for the way he created you. Thank him for redeeming you and adopting you into his family, as a person of ultimate worth.

For Further Reading:
Maurice Wagner, *The Sensation of Being Somebody* (Zondervan)
Josh McDowell, *Your Image—His Image* (Here's Life)

11
Learning to Like Myself

TORRE WAS BORN WITH A SERIOUS CLEFT PALATE and hairlip. His father, a wealthy contractor, spared no expense in helping his son with plastic surgery. By the time I met Torre when he was eighteen, you had to look long and hard at his upper lip to see any remaining sign of a scar. But Torre knew it was there, and as a result, he did not like himself and thought others felt the same.

After a long struggle with the Holy Spirit, Torre committed himself to Christ—but he didn't grow, he didn't change. He tried, but nothing worked. Because he still disliked himself, he became a person who created trouble wherever he went. He could not trust God because he felt God had made a mess of him when he was born and he didn't like the results. The last I heard of Torre, he was struggling with a serious drinking problem and slowly sliding down the road to destruction.

It's difficult to like or trust God when you don't like yourself. The attitude you have toward yourself plays a major role in forming your attitude toward God. If you don't like yourself, chances are good that you'll have a hard time liking or trusting God.

This might not appear to be a problem. How many people are there who don't like themselves? Over half the population. At least that is what psychologists estimate. People don't like themselves because they reject the "givens" in their lives, the things they can't change. They don't like the way they look. They don't like the abilities they have—or more likely don't have. They don't like their parents or the surroundings in which they grew up. They reject all or some of these things and in the process end up rejecting themselves.

Adjustment Problems

Lack of self-acceptance creates major adjustment problems.

First, *if we don't like ourselves we're unable to trust God.* There's a reason for that. Subconsciously we think, "God is the one who is responsible for creating me as I am and placing me where I grew up. Since I don't like the way I look, the abilities I have, and the situation I grew up in, *God can't be trusted.*" This was Torre's problem.

Maybe you feel God played a dirty trick on you. You

don't see him as a loving heavenly Father looking out for your needs.

How do you see God? As a cruel tyrant, capriciously toying with you for his own sadistic pleasure? And to prove your reasoning is right, you use your life and environment as a prime example.

Christians often compound this problem. They come to God at conversion anticipating monumental changes in their lives. Many are misled by zealous clergymen or friends who imply that they will experience instantaneous changes. However the changes God plans to accomplish in their lives will happen not only throughout their lives here on earth, but in eternity as well.

Many new Christians expect conversion to make them instantly beautiful, successful, and talented. When these things don't happen quickly, they may retain their initial commitment to Christ but will resist all future commitments. Or in their disappointment, they may become bitter and turn away from the Lord, feeling that God can't be trusted with their lives.

Second, *the person who doesn't like himself resists authority over his life*. Some of us are deeply frustrated by the things we can't control in our lives. We frequently say (or think), "I wouldn't have so many problems today if only (I wasn't so fat, God gave me more talent, my parents did a better job with me, I didn't grow up in such a rotten place)."

If you are frustrated with your life and the situation in which you live, you may be living with submerged anger. Maybe it has made you bitter toward all authority and basically distrustful of anyone who wants to control your life. Maybe the focus of your anger is a parent. Or a spouse. Or a boss. Or maybe it's God. And since God is ultimately responsible for putting you where you are, your anger at him increases with every day. The only person you feel you can trust is yourself. Well, sometimes. All other people have to be treated with caution, particularly those in authority, those with power.

Third, *lack of self-acceptance creates difficulty in interpersonal relationships*. Why? Because we're always wondering what others are thinking about us. Whenever we're near others we wonder how they're judging our appearance—the way we're dressed, our facial features (maybe you hate your Streisand nose!), our body shape, or our talents—how we compare with others in the group or our own family members.

We imagine that people are always looking at us and judging us. To be quite frank, most people aren't looking at us because their own self-centeredness causes them to be wondering what others are thinking about them. Thus shyness or self-consciousness is really a form of pride. We imagine that every time we walk into a group we're on center stage with a spotlight beaming down so everyone can examine us.

Sharon, a seventh-grader, took increasingly longer periods of time putting on her makeup before she left for school each morning. It never quite went just the way she wanted it. Most of the time her father patiently waited, but she'd already made him late for work a couple of times this week. When he asked her to hurry, she said,

"But Daddy, I want to look just right when I get to school so no one will laugh at me."

Her father looked at her a moment before saying, "You are proud, aren't you?"

Sharon looked shocked. "Proud? What are you talking about? I'm not proud."

"Sure you are," her father continued, "because you think all the other kids in school are going to be waiting for you to appear so they can see if you got your makeup on right this morning. They don't have anything else to do but wait for you."

Suddenly, Sharon saw what her father was talking about.

Fourth, *when we don't accept ourselves, we accept unbiblical standards of achievement.* We try to earn acceptance with others and God by our achievements. We're afraid people won't like us if they get to know us, so we fake it. We pretend to be the type of person we think they will like and accept into their group. But this puts us into an uncomfortable double bind. When others finally accept us, we know in our heart of hearts that the person they like isn't really who we are. As a result we continue to live with nagging doubts, "If they really knew me as I am they wouldn't like me, and that's all I've got." So fail or succeed, we still don't achieve the goal we set out to accomplish.

Many people use their achievements to hide their defects. They reason, "If I perform beyond anyone else, then other people (and God) won't notice all the bad things about me." But God already knows all about us. When we try to hide from him by putting on a show of our goodness, we keep him from effectively dealing with the very defects that shame us. The Holy Spirit can't work until we're willing to admit we need his help.

Finally, *when we don't accept ourselves, we become materialistic*. Our materialism compensates for the deficiencies we feel we have in our lives and personalities. We think, "If I can't be what I want, at least I can buy things that make me happy." So we spend money to make up for the lacks in our lives. Spending money does feel good, but in the end it cannot achieve what we seek.

We often use money not so much to buy happiness for ourselves as to achieve status with others. This is why so many people want to go out and get the latest *whatever*. It's not that they need it, but that if they don't have it they might fall behind and not keep up with everyone else. The race is never-ending because there's always something new that is the status symbol for this week.

Stepping Toward Self-Acceptance

If self-acceptance is so important, what's the solution to our dilemma? It sounds so simple we hesitate to state it. Most people have heard it so often that they discount it. What is it?

Self-acceptance begins with a personal relationship with Jesus Christ. We cannot accept ourselves for who we are until we ask Jesus to be our Savior and become enfolded in his arms. Then we know he loves us exactly as we are—crooked noses, bulging stomachs, duck feet, and all.

Once we establish a relationship with Jesus, self-acceptance comes more easily. We discover, "I can now love myself because God, *who fully knows me,* loves me!" The importance of this for self-acceptance is staggering. No one knows more about you than the Holy Spirit. There is nothing about your life, thoughts, or actions that you can hide from him (Psalm 139:1-5). Yet he loves you. When you don't like yourself, you live in constant fear that others might really get to know you and reject you as a result. But when you come to God, you come to someone who already knows you and loves you anyway. If this great and wonderful God loves you, how can you reject yourself?

There's more. The Holy Spirit has promised to meet every legitimate need you have for all eternity (Romans 8:32). With that sort of support, you can now focus your attention on others' lives. You don't have to worry about how others are going to respond to your appearance, abilities, or background. Instead you can focus on their needs because the Holy Spirit has taken care of any problems that might result from those things that used to bother you.

We also need to thank God for the unchangeable "givens" in our lives. This requires a turn-around for many of us. But our faith in Christ should bring us to this point. God is now our loving heavenly Father. He has always been our Creator, knowing we would come to him as Savior. Now we can see that he acted in love when he created us. By his loving wisdom, and for his eternal glory, he created us just as we are. He knew what we would face during our lives, he knew the temptations and areas of service that would challenge us. As a result he created us with an appearance, abilities, and gave us the parents and surroundings we needed to perfectly fit us for the life he wanted us to lead and use as a ministry for him. What we used to view as a cruel joke is now seen as an act of love.

Let's look specifically at each of the unchangeable elements, the givens.

1. *We need to thank God for the "defects" in our appearance.* Maybe you have a nose that could be used as a ski slope; maybe you are shaped less like an hourglass and more like a bowling pin; maybe each time the sun comes out you have to cover your head to keep from blinding people—I don't know what your "defect" might be. I do know, however, that you need to thank God for it. In doing this you acknowledge that he is a sovereign, loving God and that by faith you trust him that he did the best job possible in creating you. Until you thank him for your "defects," you'll never fully accept yourself and find true freedom.

Many people struggle with God's love in creating us with "defects." They assume these can be nothing other than the work of Satan.

Moses knew he couldn't be a speaker. He'd spent his whole life shadowed by his older brother Aaron, a dynamic kind of guy who seemed to be good at everything. And yet God asked him to carry an important message of freedom to his people. Moses couldn't believe that God had asked *him*.

"Why didn't you ask my brother?" Moses asked God incredulously.

God has a good argument for Moses in Exodus 4. "Who

makes mouths?" Jehovah asked him. "Isn't it I, the Lord? Who makes a man so that he can speak or not speak, see or not see, hear or not hear?"

God asserts that he created the blind, the deaf, and the mute. If he assumes responsibility for these "calamities" can't we also see his hand in our "defects?" And see them as acts of love from an all-knowing, mighty God who is personally in touch with each of us?

2. *We also need to thank God for the "defects" in our abilities*. The Bible teaches us that the Holy Spirit gives each of us gifts for life and service (1 Corinthians 12:4-7). This means he gives each of us precisely the abilities we need to both serve him and get along in life. If that's the case, it also means he has deliberately withheld certain talents from us because he knew we either would not need them or would abuse them.

If you were a Miss America contestant you might like the cheering of the crowd and not hear God's call on your life. If you had abilities that brought you fame and fortune, like being a rock singer or a professional football player, you might never realize your poverty before God. In love God gifted you. You now need to thank him both for the gifts you have and for the gifts he withheld, because each is a result of his loving wisdom.

You may wish you were more of a warm, vivacious person. Instead you're shy, and a bit reserved. Doing things in front of groups is painful for you. But God gave you a gift for helping hurting individuals. And you just discovered you're a wonderful listener when others have problems. What a wonderful, rare gift God has given you!

3. *We also need to thank God for the homes we grew*

up in. Many of us understand the need to thank God for appearance and abilities, but we rebel in this area. We may have been psychologically or physically abused in our homes. Maybe our homes smelled of alcohol and stale vomit because of a parent's drinking problem.

How can you thank God for the abuse that was part of your home, the almost daily pain and suffering that came from living there, the open wounds you still carry along with the pain? There's no way you'll thank God for that!

But hold on. Is God really a God of love who is also in control? If so, we need to thank him—for pain as well as success and joy.

If your parents were perfect, you might be so well-adjusted that you might not realize you need help from outside yourself. If the environment where you grew up was not seriously flawed, you might be content to stay there for the rest of your life.

After months of counseling, one man told me, "I realize now that it was my home life as a child that developed my cool emotional response to life. I can fight that and complain about it, or I can thank God for the good that was also there and recognize he had a purpose that I may never fully understand—but he did it out of love." With that recognition, the man began to work consciously on his relationships with his wife and children in his own home. And the home was transformed step by step.

The Holy Spirit placed us in the homes where we grew up. We had nothing to do with choosing them ourselves. When we know that God is both loving and all-powerful, we must realize that he must have had a reason for letting us be born where we were. He knows the future before us. He knows what we will be called to do and the people we will come in contact with.

The home is the school where God prepares us for service. The abuse, the pain we felt in growing up in our families, prepared us to minister in Jesus' name to others. Had we not had those experiences, our ministry would be sharply curtailed. In realizing this, we have reason to thank God even for our home life, no matter how difficult or painful.

4. *Finally, we need to thank God for the defects in our surroundings.* Whether you grew up as the wealthy child of a leading member of the community, or a pastor's kid in a church where people watched your every move, or in a poverty-stricken area of the Bronx, or in an abusive home, God was there. He knew not only what you went through, but also how all of that would fit into your future. He guided each step you took so you would be prepared to serve him in a ministry, especially designed just for you. He placed you with loving care in your surroundings.

After we've thanked God for all his concern for us, we need to commit ourselves to cooperating with his plans for the rest of our lives. We certainly aren't perfect. There are many flaws in our characters. Sometimes we rebel, take detours of our own choosing, and bear the scars for our choices. But the Holy Spirit wants to work in our lives to recreate the character of Jesus Christ. He made us as we are so he could use us in his service. Now God plans to bring us to perfection, a process that begins at conversion and continues into eternity. We need to submit our lives to his will and seek his guidance for the rest of our lives.

A New Kind of Freedom

What happens when you finally accept yourself for who you are? Your life is dramatically changed.

You gain freedom and closeness in your walk with God like you've never known before. Now you can love and trust him because you know it was his love, not his cruelty, that made you who you are. Now you can come to him with all your faults exposed and seek his help in changing them. As a result of this new openness on your part, he will be able to work far more effectively and quickly than ever before.

Self-acceptance enables you to enter deeper, more satisfying personal relationships. You can now focus on others' needs rather than on their opinions of you. When you do that you'll be astonished at how people respond to you. Many of us are afraid that truly living as a Christian will cut us off from others, but look at Christ's life! He was a man who did everything God wanted, and the crowds flocked after him during his three-year ministry. As we follow him and focus on others' needs, God will truly bless our lives and ministries as well.

Self-acceptance means you become comfortable with both your strengths and your weaknesses. As I counseled a woman whose daughter kept an unbelievably sloppy room I asked her, "When you were a teen, what did your mother think of the way you kept your room?"

She looked straight at me and said, "If you ever let my daughter know how messy my room was as a teen, I'll . . ." And she sputtered in rage.

This woman was still carrying her past before her and it was affecting her relationship with her daughter. She wanted her daughter to be something even she couldn't be at that age. Perhaps explaining to her daughter what she was like at that age herself would have brought a few chuckles, a hug, and renewed understanding between mother and daughter.

Most of us want to operate from a position of strength, but again and again the Bible tells us that God's strength is perfected through our weaknesses. Admitting we have weaknesses ourselves makes more honest relationships. It allows your friend, spouse, child, or leader to be just what you are—less than perfect. We can be just as comfortable with our weaknesses as our strengths.

Finally, *self-acceptance gives you less concern about things and more concern for people.* On a practical level it makes it easier to balance your budget because you won't need to get the latest gadget on the market. Your self-acceptance gives you the assurance to resist many foolish purchases. You don't have to compensate for what you aren't or what you don't have. By accepting who you are, you'll have less need than before to accumulate unnecessary possessions, and more time for the people who are important to you.

The answer to self-acceptance is simple—and yet difficult. But if we want to implement these principles, we should act now. Our low opinion of ourselves quickly reasserts itself unless we act on each suggestion. By committing yourself fully to Jesus Christ and to doing his will for the rest of your life, you can learn to thank him—for who you are, where you've come from, where you're going, and for what you are going to do together as you daily learn more about yourself and serving him.

Things to Do/Think About:
1. What difficulties do you face because you don't accept yourself?
2. What steps can you take to gain self-acceptance?
3. What changes do you anticipate in your life as you learn to accept yourself?
4. If you have kept your thoughts from this book on paper or in a journal, glance through them from beginning to end. What changes have you seen in your self-talk? in the way you value yourself? others? God?

For Further Reading:
Bruce Narramore, *You're Someone Special* (Zondervan)